Number 14

Hot Rodding
INTERNATIONAL

Contents

AF251619

Front cover photo: From the Kevin Mayo Collection. The Mayo Collection is featured this issue, starting on page 50.

Published in 2022 by Graffiti Publications Pty. Ltd.
69 Forest Street, Castlemaine, 3450, Victoria, Australia.
Phone International: +61 3 5472 3653 or +61 3 5472 3805.
Email: info@graffitipub.com.au
Website: www.graffitipub.com.au
Publisher/Editor: Larry O'Toole.
Text & Production: Larry O'Toole, Al O'Toole, Mary-Anna Brennand.
Sales & Marketing: Mary O'Toole, Wendy Thomas.
Photos: Larry O'Toole, Al O'Toole, Greg Stokes, Mark Bach, Peter Max, Kevin Mayo, Paul Northey, Gerry Burger, Les Winter, Charlie Smith, Nick Darling, Marcus Ohms.

The information in this publication is true and complete to the best of our knowledge. All recommendations are made without any guarantee on the part of the author or publisher, who also disclaim any liability incurred in connection with the use of this data or specific details.

We recognise that some words, model names and designations mentioned herein, are the property of the trademark holder. We use them for identification purposes only. This is not an official publication.

Graffiti Publications titles are also available at discounts in bulk quantity for industrial or sales promotional use. For details contact Graffiti Publications Ph: (613) 5472 3653. Printed & bound in Singapore by SC (Sang Choy) International Pte Ltd. ISSN: 1836-2850. ISBN: 978-0-949398-85-7

Introduction

My Hot Rodding Life...

Something different this time around. I have spent my whole life deeply involved in hot rodding and more particularly in the publishing of books and magazines like the one you are reading now. I built my first hot rod when I was only 19 years of age from the Model A Ford shown here. In fact it was the first car I owned. I have been at it ever since. COVID-19 changed the world for everyone and we aren't exempt on that score, so we had to find different ways to accomplish what we do for a living – publish magazines. Through all the years since we started in this business (47, but who's counting) we have maintained an extensive archive by keeping and indexing everything we covered in the magazines. That meant we could draw on much unpublished material while the pandemic restricted our movement and thus the ability to gather new material in our usual ways. So it was that when considering what content we could gather together for this issue, we had an in-house discussion about my own life in hot rodding. When you are so deeply involved for such a long time it is easy to take only a cursory account of what you have done yourself. It didn't take long to realise that we were sitting on a treasure trove of hot rodding nostalgia that has emanated from within my own backyard workshop.

The result is a different Introduction piece for this issue. Normally contained to only these two pages, this time we have expanded it into a whole retrospective of my own hot rod building activities over the past 50 years. Starting out with my upbringing on a Victorian Mallee wheat farm, where I built my first hot rod, and tracing a life of project cars all the way to today, coincidentally a time when I am actually re-creating that first hot rod project. I hope you enjoy the read. ◼

MY HOT RODDING LIFE...

Words & Photos: Larry & Al O'Toole

ABOVE: This picture should tell you plenty about my farm upbringing, yes a lot of chooks, turkeys, sheep, cows and wheat. That's me in the foreground at about age eight or nine pushing the bulldozer. Younger brother, Geoff is on the right and neighbour John Thomas from across the road.

G rowing up in the Victorian Mallee was no different for me than every other farm raised child where we were exposed to lots of farm machinery and animals. We lived blissfully ignorant of what most of the rest of the world was doing and never travelled far from home, especially prior to about age 10. When I was not much older than a toddler I can recall getting birthday and Christmas gifts that were very often items of toy farming equipment, so the exposure to mechanical things was there from a very early age.

That exposure to full scale mechanical things always had me fascinated in how they worked and I often had to use such equipment when helping out during school holidays. In fact I was driving tractors at age 7 when I was just a wisp of a boy, so much so that to engage the clutch I had to stand up on the pedal to gain enough leverage to make it operate. Leisure time was consumed by the activity we always called car camps, where we played with Dinky toys for hours on end and built whole farming

LEFT: At the wheel of "The Big A" as we dubbed it at the time. House paint was used to brush paint the vehicle blue with white highlights and "pinstriping" around the edges of the panels. We thought it was rather daring to add the Roth style cartoon with "Thou Shalt Drag" and "Help Promote Street Racing" messages.

ABOVE: In 1963 my father bought a brand new XL Falcon ute, just the basic model with 144 engine, but I felt like a king driving that brand new ute around the farm. That's me and dad standing at the back of the ute. The engine didn't last all that long so dad bought a Repco changeover unit and I was offered the job of fitting it – had it done in less than a day! Note the wheat truck in the background.

BELOW: Bulk handling of wheat became popular in the early sixties, so I often drove this Bedford truck to the local silo. A friend sent me this photo recently after he stumbled across the truck, still sitting semi-derelict on a Mallee farm at Chinkapook.

BELOW: The original Model A bucket was built from the roadster that had been converted to a ute as shown on the introduction page. It was built in that farm shed in the background of this photo on a single section of concrete floor just large enough for the car to sit on. That's Mary in the driver's seat at 18 years of age. All the running gear came from a '48 Mercury that I purchased from Castlemaine.

communities in miniature. Every month or so there would be a shopping trip to Swan Hill for the larger items or farm equipment and that's when I would get the chance to visit Slater's Sports Store the local supplier of Dinky, Corgi and Matchbox toys.

Once I entered my teenage years, the farm work often took on a more major aspect and eventually to driving our old Bedford truck that came along in the early sixties when most wheat farmers started using bulk handling equipment. Dad bought the Bedford from the local garage that specialised in bringing tarted-up trucks from Melbourne to sell to the cockies. Ours had been a Coca-Cola truck (repainted grey) and was well-travelled (read gutless, especially with a 300 bag load of wheat on board). Once I had my licence I used to often drive it to the silos while dad continued working on the header.

In 1963 dad bought a brand new XL Falcon ute for the farm. He had previously bought his first brand new car in 1959 – a '59 MkII Zephyr, everything prior to that was second hand, including a '37 Chev, '48 Oldsmobile and an FX Holden ute. I thought it was amazing being able to drive a brand new Falcon ute around the farm and did so at every opportunity.

During this same period an A Model Ford ute, that was purchased from a next door neighbour when he sold up and got out of farming, entered my life. The neighbour and dad used to spray the crops with it, he owned the ute, dad owned the spray mister machine. It was ideal for this purpose as it didn't get bogged on the sand hills and would chug away for hours at a constant speed using the hand throttle.

I wanted to drive the A Model around the farm but it had no brakes – dad said fix the brakes and you can use it – done in 20 minutes! This vehicle had been a roadster but was cut into a ute with an axe down the length of the quarter panels that were then nailed to the wooden sides of the ute back.

Together with my best friend, Frank Punch we painted the A Model with Moon-eyes and Roth cartoons, plus pinstriped around each panel. We had a lot of fun and learnt the basics of vehicle handling at the same time. It had a chopped windscreen and lowered front suspension, apparently done by a previous owner some time in the pre '50s era. This was possibly done to make it look more like a '32, as the bumpers were bolted together without the spacers and then reshaped to resemble '32 bumpers.

I spent school days at boarding college in Bendigo dreaming of and drawing cars. The library was a favourite spot, just so I could look at the car adverts in National Geographic – Caddies, Pontiacs, Buicks, Fords and even Holdens. How I dreamt of one day owning such a vehicle!

I remember an incident in English class when I was in Form 4 quite clearly, as it had a direct affect on my future life. Fr O'Keefe was our English teacher and he was a very tall, commanding man, who didn't stand for any nonsense in class. He caught me drawing a picture of a wheel in class and decided to make an example of my folly. He held up the drawing before the class and asked what it was. I replied, "A racing car." "It doesn't look like a racing car," he scoffed. "Well it will if you let me finish it," was my reply. Of course I wasn't going to win the argument. "Where do you think drawing pictures of cars in English class will get you in life?" He added.

Fr O'Keefe was actually a very good English teacher and it was my best subject at school, but there was a heart-warming revisitation of this story many, many years later. I found out about 10 years ago that Fr O'Keefe was still alive (in his late 80s) and living in a retirement home in Sydney, so I sent him a copy of the magazine with a note attached that read; "This is where drawing pictures of cars in your English class got me in life!" He saw the funny side of it and wrote back a nice letter, ending with the statement, "I will look on hot rods in a whole different light now." Sadly, he passed away a few years later.

I started going out with Mary in May '68 and set about building the A Model ute into a hot rod at about the same time. I pulled it apart with a view to restoring it, but lots of it was really bad, so I decided to attempt a hot rod and turned it into my bucket. For this first project I used the cowl and doors, added tourer rear doors and welded them all together. Then I framed the rear with light box tube steel and filled in the panels across the back with sheet metal. I kept the bonnet, valance panels, guards and bonnet off the ute and the valances are now on my Model A Tudor.

The bucket was built in a farm shed on a single slab of concrete floor not much bigger than the car. We had welders in the shed, but not much else.

I bought a complete '48 Mercury sedan from Castlemaine and pulled it apart, just to get the running gear for the bucket, because a neighbour wouldn't sell me his dead Customline with Y block engine. All the mechanical components and suspension out of the Mercury went in the bucket, but I kept the body and chassis, which later came with me to Castlemaine. That car later became a rod as well and is still on the road.

As I built the bucket I test drove it around the farm yard with fuel tin and battery on the front floor and the leads and fuel line draped over the windscreen to the engine.

The Krahnert Brothers of Swan Hill built their T bucket at the same time. We lived in Gray Street Swan Hill at the time and so did they, so we were always checking on each other's project. Both finished within a week or two of each other, mine registered without the interior trim done, but completed soon after by a neighbour who was a trimmer.

The bucket was painted a HQ Holden Premier colour – gold but I wasn't impressed with how it turned out – it looked too plain,

so I added stick-on woodgrain that led to pattern painting in purple over the gold for a much better looking result.

As it turned out, the Merc engine was no good, it had a burnt valve, so I bought a hot flathead from Sydney that was built by Brian Hynes. It had only been drag raced to that point and it was really fast for a sidevalve. In fact, I broke the National Drag Record for D/HR class with it at the Moomba Nationals in 1971.

The bucket was my first car, but soon after finishing it Mary and I bought our first "normal" car, a '63 Austin Freeway sedan. It wasn't a bad car, but had a badly slipping clutch due to a leaking rear main. I put up with it until I traded it on the blue XP hardtop that we used for the next couple of years. We thrashed the daylights out of it, making a fast trip to Perth and back in it, competing in rallies etc. We traded it on an XY Falcon ute just before moving to Castlemaine in July 1973, but I always hankered to own another XP hardtop in the future.

We also owned a '64 Galaxie at that time, bought for $300.00 from the local Chrysler dealer where it had been traded in by a visiting caravanner, as the transmission was playing up. I swapped in another transmission and drove the Galaxie everywhere for the next few years. It had a really good 390 in it and could easily cruise at 100 mph (you could do that on desolate back roads in those days).

One day I had been burning around town (Swan Hill) in the bucket in 1970 when I blew the gearbox at the front gate of the house where we were living on Mary's brother's fruit block, so I decided to do a complete rebuild. I sold the old rolling chassis to a bloke in Sea Lake and built a new 3x2 box tube chassis in a weekend, using a tube axle I made on the floor and a Mainline Ambulance widened rear end (it had two inch blocks added to each end of the axle housings to give it a wider track). I adapted a six cylinder Torqueflite transmission to the flathead with my own adaptor. Initially it wouldn't drive because I had miscalculated on the crankshaft to flexplate adaptor and the torque converter wasn't engaging in the transmission. I took it apart and reversed the curved flex plate to fix the problem and it drove perfectly.

We used the XP hardtop to tow the rebuilt bucket to the Sydney Hot Rod Show in 1972; at the time I hadn't even driven the bucket in its new metalflake painted form, as I had yet to fix the no-drive issue. We borrowed Ken Spence's trailer to tow it and had a freak accident north of Deniliquin when the trailer separated from the XP tow car. It turned out that the safety chains were attached to the bolt-on towing tongue and when the bolts rattled out the whole rolling package was separated from the XP, just that we didn't know that at the time. The trailer towed so well that it followed the XP perfectly, occasionally bumping against the back of the car, because I thought it was still hanging on

ABOVE: Older brother Bernie and younger brother Geoff contemplate the folly of a young hot rodder about to go a for a test drive around the farm yard. The battery sat on the front floor alongside a one gallon can of fuel with leads and fuel line under the windscreen. First drive was exciting!

TOP: Embarking on the first test drive was the culmination of a big day for a 19 year-old.

ABOVE: The original Model A roadster that had been cut down to a ute, shown from the left side that featured Rat Fink and Mooneyes logo done in an afternoon using house paint. I am about 16 years of age in this photo.

LEFT: In the background is the Krahnert brothers' T bucket that was built at the same time with 352 Ford engine. This is just after registration as my bucket has no interior trim. It was added soon after.

BELOW: The Krahnert bucket was hand made using a Dodge cowl and Model A rear of front seat panel with formed sheet metal sides. The late Dick Krahnert in the driver's seat with then soon to be wife Michelle standing.

ABOVE: Soon after registration the stock Mercury flathead was replaced with this hot version that I bought from Lindsay Harris in Sydney. The hot flathead was built by David Hynes and it was very fast for its time, having only been drag raced until I bought it. The purple lace paint was added to spark the appearance up a bit. In this form the bucket held the National D/HR Drag Racing Record for nine months, having set it at the '71 Moomba Nationals at Calder Raceway.
BELOW: Our first XP Falcon was this blue hardtop that we bought while still living in Swan Hill. Even though it was our everyday car we drove it hard, competed in rallies and made a trip to Perth and back in it in 1972, when there were still 500 miles of rough gravel road to endure, hence Mary kissing the bitumen at the end of that section. Temperature was in the 40° C region for most of the trip.

ABOVE & RIGHT: Having destroyed the Mercury three speed manual gearbox, I decided to rebuild the whole car, finishing it in three shades of metalflake with pattern painted panels and adapting a six cylinder Torqueflite automatic transmission to the hot flathead. I also replaced the modified Model A chassis with a box tube item I made in one weekend and chromed almost everything that would unbolt. Taillights were updated using Datsun items and coil spring rear suspension added to a unique, widened Mainline diff that came from an ambulance.

the chains. I can tell you my heart jumped into my mouth when we started rounding a gentle corner in the road and the trailer slid past the passenger side of the XP. The trailer and the bucket were then in the hands of fate. Fortunately it careered between the white posts without hitting any of them and as it went off the edge of the road was headed straight at a power pole when the tow bar dug in and it all came to a halt with no damage! Nothing was said for several minutes as we absorbed what had just happened. I drove back to Deniliquin for new bolts and checked that tow bar every 20 miles, or so it seemed, from there to Sydney.

After the drama encountered on the trip up we came home very happy with Second Bucket and Top Metalflake paint awards from our first big show.

Where I worked at the Swan Hill Guardian, there was a printer who was also into cars a bit, but later models in particular. One day he came into work and told me there was an old roadster amongst a heap of cars on the property next door to where he lived. His description sounded very much like it was a '32 Ford roadster, but I thought, "Nah, couldn't be, but let's check it out anyway." The rest of the cars all sounded like they were '34 Chev sedans. He enquired of the neighbour who told him they had removed the engine from it many years previous to use on a sawbench and they didn't want it, so we were welcome to come and get it if we liked. The next day an inspection was made and lo and behold, it was a '32 roadster. I couldn't get it loaded onto a trailer quick enough! Even though it was in quite sad condition, with most of the wood smouldered out of it from burning off, but I could see that it was salvageable. It turned out the rest of the cars in the dump were in fact '34 Chev sedans as well. I have no idea if anything was ever done about rescuing them as I wasn't interested in them.

It was about this time that I started looking for a Model A Tudor as that was the next rod I wanted to build. The search took me all over Victoria and I did eventually find a body only, but considered it too expensive at $100.00. Would you believe I eventually unearthed one only about six miles from our farm and was able to purchase the body, four fenders and grille shell for $45.00 – that was more like the going price at the time. I started

ABOVE: Posed photo was for the local paper after returning home from breaking the National Drag Record at Calder Park Raceway during the Moomba Nationals in March 1971.

ABOVE: The '32 Ford roadster was picked up off the ground from a farm near Swan Hill after I was alerted to it by a workmate. It was fairly sad but did have all body repairs completed and the basic chassis built before it was shelved. I still have it and hope to complete it – one day!

making up my own chassis and suspension for the Tudor when fate stepped in.

We attended the first Street Rod Nationals in Narrandera in 1973, towing the bucket there on a trailer because I couldn't get it to run cool enough to drive all the way. I couldn't believe it when some rodders called out "trailer sailor" when we drove past – I had never heard the term before then. Very few of my cars have ever been on a trailer since, none when finished unless broken down!

On the return trip from Narrandera I was troubled by a problem with my right eye that was soon diagnosed as conjunctivitis. It actually turned out much worse then that and was in fact caused by an infection directly over the pupil of my eye. Three months of treatment under a specialist and no work followed, as I almost lost the sight in that eye. While I was off work (as a photographer and pre-print specialist for the local paper) I travelled up and down to Castlemaine to visit with Eddie Ford whom I had got to know since he called in on us in Swan Hill while on a vintage tin hunt. The result was that I never returned to my newspaper job and we made arrangements to move to Castlemaine, me to go to work on Custom Rodder magazine and Mary into the Pharmacy Assistant's job at Alexander, the Castlemaine aged home.

Before leaving Swan Hill to move to Castlemaine I bought a 283 Chevy from a racing boat for $110.00, almost all the spare cash I had at the time. I left behind two tea chests full of flathead speed equipment because I didn't have the additional $30.00 to buy it! It all went to scrap. The 283 had a homemade intake with twin two barrel Holleys and was balanced etc, so it went really well (14.5 at drags at Calder). I fitted a stock Chevy four barrel manifold and put an alloy Powerglide behind it. This running gear was swapped into the bucket in 1974 and I then sold the flathead and Torqueflite.

Moving to Castlemaine was like going to heaven for a young hot rodder. Because I had been working as a newspaper photographer and pre-press specialist at the time and didn't realise how much benefit that experience would be later in life.

At the time we had only been married two years and moving

ABOVE: I hadn't even driven the rebuilt bucket when we decided to tow it to Sydney for the 1972 Hot Rod Show at Roselands. Just out of Deniliquin the trailer parted ways with the towing XP and went past us on the left side, only stopping when the trailer's drawbar dug into the ground as it left the road and headed straight for a power pole! Bolts holding the tow bar tongue had rattled out and let it drop to the road, taking the safety chains with it!

LEFT & ABOVE: Gleaming colour slides of the bucket in the Sydney show really shows up the tri-colour metalflake paintwork that took weeks to apply. Note the unfinished exhaust and Skog wheels. The carpark venue at Roselands where the show as held was a very dark place.

LEFT: Before we left Swan Hill and moved to Castlemaine in 1973, I bought this hot 283 Chevy engine from the son of a boat racer after his father had passed away. This was an early 283 with staggered bolt rocker covers and was a strong engine. It went very well in the bucket with quarter mile times of 14.5 seconds (unfortunately against Dave Gale in the Baroness). The twin two barrel carbies were mounted on a manifold fabricated from sheet steel. I changed it to a standard Chevy four barrel. At lower left the Chevy is fitted in the bucket an we are participating in the street parade at the Narrandera Nationals in 1975. Yes, I had hair then!

RIGHT: Just back from the Sydney Hot Rod Show in 1972 with trophies for Top Metalflake Paint and Second in Bucket class. Another photo for the local paper where I worked as the press photographer at the time. Mary worked nearby in the office of a local engineering firm, and then in the pharmacy at the hospital

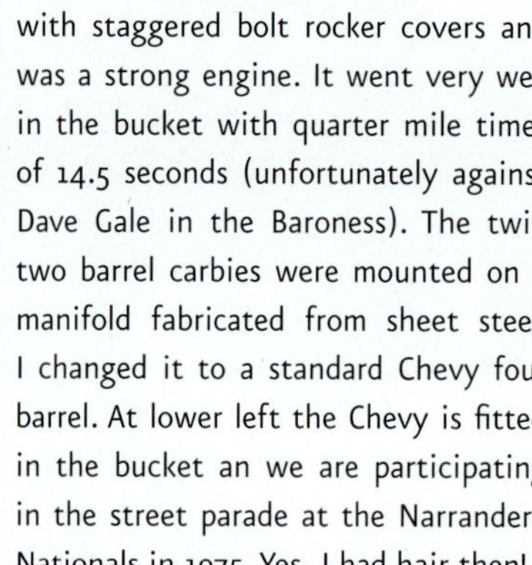

Photo by Mick Dunne

was like stepping off a cliff, but being young and having a sense of adventure gave us the courage to make the move. The house we were going to rent sold just before we moved and no other was available, so I raced around and bought the house we live in today and we moved into it all, in the space of four days! Mary scored the job as pharmacy assistant at the Alexander Home for the Aged, so we were able to pull it off and start what has been a wonderful life of our own in a place we soon grew to love immensely – the best thing we ever did!

I brought the Bucket, the Model A Tudor and the '32 roadster with me to Castlemaine and even started work on the roadster some time later. It appeared in ASR several times as tech articles and then I lost interest due to taking on too many other projects, so it went on the back-burner – it's still there!

The job with Eddie had been great but by late '74 it was clear it wasn't going to be permanent, so I started looking for an alternative. I saw an auction notice for a photographic business in the Castlemaine cbd and bought almost everything with our meagre savings so we could set up our own photographic business. It struggled for two or three years until we moved into the main street and saw the turnover triple in one year.

In 1976 we formed Graffiti Publications when myself and three other partners launched Australian Street Rodding magazine. The first issue was published in time for release at the 1977 ASRF Nationals in Narrandera.

We sold the bucket in 1975 to have enough money to finish the Model A Tudor that I had brought with me from Swan Hill as a just started project. It was built in the tiny shed and backyard at home and finished just in time for the Victorian State Rod Run in Castlemaine, March 1976. I used a 396 big block Chevy with Powerglide transmission that was purchased from Jack Kavanagh in Preston, used the homemade 4x2 chassis that I started in Swan Hill and added Torana front end and Tank Fairlane nine inch diff on Torana coils and four link. Those components are still all there today, having travelled around 300,000 miles and all been completely reconditioned about 20 years ago when I converted it to straight LPG. Many of its earlier miles were clocked up pulling a homemade trailer (based on a repro pickup bed) so we could take along everything needed for a growing family. The Model A Tudor appeared as a series of tech articles in Custom Rodder at the time 1974-1976.

By late in the seventies the Model A Tudor was completed and in regular service and for some time was used as our family car. As our economic situation improved I decided I would like to fulfill a lifetime dream to own a big two door American car. I wasn't too fussy about the brand, I just wanted another big American car like the '64 Galaxie I had when we first moved to Castlemaine. I responded to an advertisement for a '65 Chev

and '63 Oldsmobile in Bayswater, Vic. When I turned up at the factory address the owner tried to push me toward the four door Olds, but I was set on the Chevy as it was a two door Belair. It was in fair condition, registered and drivable but did have some rust in the floor of the boot as it had been used to tow racing boats. Although it had originally been 327 powered, it was fitted with a warmed over, but rattly 283 that had obviously done a lot of miles. Nevertheless I couldn't wait to get it home and rebuild it from end to end, although that had to wait while we saved up some more money.

A rebuilder 327 engine with fuellie heads was purchased from Rob Muston at Motion Speed Shop in Bendigo and the late Mick Farrell gave it a freshen up with bore, cam, head port etc., before it was mated to an alloy Powerglide and fitted into the Chev. While that was happening I stripped the body, fixed the rust and painted it Statesman Mandarin Red, that was actually closer to orange than red, fitted a set of alloy wheels and trimmed the interior using woollen material made at the local woollen

ABOVE: The blue XP was traded for this ex-shire, six cylinder XY Falcon ute that was barely 12 months old. Nobody recognised us in the ute because it was plain white, so I decide to add some colour. The ute came to Castlemaine with us and was later rebuilt with V8 running gear by another owner.

mill. We then used it as our everyday family car for some time, but I did remove the 327, as it was using copious amounts of oil, and replaced it with a John Cain Saturday Night Special 350. On tearing the 327 down I discovered that the hard racing rings fitted when it was rebuilt had polished the bores, but otherwise it was still in good condition. I set it aside for a future project (the current Model A Bucket re-creation) and went on working on other projects. Mary used the Chev right up until the mid-1990s when it was put off the road by a Highway Patrol cop in about 1996 for being too low. By this time rust had become evident in the front and back windscreen openings as well as small amounts in the lower door pillars etc., so I elected to pull it down and start over again. All the rust repair work was completed and most of the car put into high-build primer when other projects and business commitments got in the way and the project stalled. It is still awaiting completion in 2021, which is a pity as it is a wonderful road car.

The magazine business struggled until we went full time on it in 1980-81. We sold the photographic business in 1981 to concentrate fully on magazine production and it started to improve rapidly. Then I decided we needed another project car to focus attention on the magazine through tech articles and since early Falcons were starting to become popular, went looking for a suitable vehicle. We located an XP Falcon panel van only about 50 metres from my own house. It was fairly rough but basically all there and once purchased and cleaned up a bit turned out to be better than first imagined. It looked bad because it was different colours with patches of primer here and there on the body. It originally had a window in each side of the "panel" but we filled them in to make it a solid sided panel van as they were

ABOVE INSET: In its first year on the road the Model A Tudor was driven to Adelaide for their hot rod show in October '76 where this photo was taken.
BELOW: The Model A Tudor was registered the same week as the first Victorian State Rod Run that was held in Castlemaine. Here it leads the run out along the Ballarat Road through Yapeen, followed by Geoff Knape's '34 Ford coupe and a line of rod run entrants.

RIGHT: Competing in the Street Rod Drags at Heathcote Park Raceway in the late seventies/early eighties. I went home with $100.00 in my pocket for winning the Hot Rod dial your own bracket, but only raced the Tudor a couple of times. It would run 15.00 all day long with stock 396 engine.

ABOVE & LEFT: Having owned the '64 Galaxie in '73-74 I decided I wanted another big American car. This rare '65 Chevy Belair two door sedan was purchased from Bayswater, Vic. and became our everyday driver for many ears. It was orignallly a 327 car but had a rattly 283 in it when we bought it. I soon stripped it down, removed much of the chrome trim, fitted a hot 327 and painted it Mandarin Red, a Holden Statesman colour that was more orange than red. It was later lowered and Mary drove it everyday until flying squad police decided it was too low and defected it. I decided on another rebuild that is yet to be completed.

considered to look better and provide space for advertising signs for the magazine. It was decided quite early in the project that we would make it a budget build that any home based enthusiast could take on, so dubbed it XP 1000 – the 1000 being the amount we anticipated spending to get it on the road i.e. $1000.00.

Back in those days the magazine was bi-monthly, and once each edition was sent to the printers we had some spare time to devote to the project car, so it progressed quite quickly. We soon had it all cleaned up and purchased a 200 cubic inch engine from an XA Falcon at the local wreckers with three speed all-synchro manual transmission for $65.00. From swap meets came front end components including XT Falcon solid disc brakes and a set of XP disc brake spindles that allowed the whole lot to bolt together for greatly improved braking.

Inside we fitted a bench seat from an XB Falcon ute that was in good condition and didn't need re-trimming. A set of popular 12 slotter wheels were fitted at all four corners to give the finished vehicle a custom, updated look. The series of articles on the vehicle proved so popular we could barely keep up to the mail (letters in those days) asking questions about it. I think we can actually take some credit for how popular these early Falcons are today, based on the amount of interest that was shown in the XP 1000 project.

Once completed (for $1350.00 - we didn't anticipate using new tyres but thought better of that plan), we used the panel van to cart our magazines and books, plus associated equipment to the hot rod shows all over the eastern half of Australia. As things got busier the loads got heavier and in the end we added air shockers to the rear end (pumped up to 90 lbs) so it could carry the enormous weight. As a result we wore out several sets of rear wheel bearings and at least three all-synchro gearboxes, plus two more later model ute seats. The engine never faltered and was given a freshen-up recondition in the late 1980s but hasn't been touched since – it still performs admirably some 250,000 miles later. XP 1000 has been rebuilt two more times since that original time back in the late '70s-early '80s (it was finished in 1982). After several years the brakes were updated to XW-XY vented discs on the XP disc brake spindles.

One day I was sitting in the office when I heard a loud bang out the front and spun around to just catch sight of the XP disappearing past the front window. An elderly lady in a Mercedes had been trying to stop a hot chicken rolling off the seat and inadvertently pulled the steering wheel at the same time, driving the Mercedes straight into the right side rear taillight of the XP van and launching it down the street. It ended up parked halfway around the corner of our office building but somehow didn't hit the building itself. There was another elderly lady in the passenger seat of the Mercedes who sustained minor injuries to her knees, but fortunately she was wearing a seat belt, preventing her from flying at full force into the dash. The Mercedes was a complete write-off back to the firewall – even the dash was bowed inward by the impact. The XP didn't fare much better – the right taillight was moved about a foot into the quarter panel and, although not readily apparent at first glance, the floor was creased right across the van between the rear wheels and the passenger area.

The only possible fix for the van was to replace the body shell, that even then wasn't an easy thing to locate. After a couple of months of looking we finally came upon an XM solid sided panel van in Colac, where it had been in storage for some 15 years. The insurance from the Mercedes owner covered the cost of purchase, plus most of the cost of repainting etc. We switched everything over from the damaged XP to the XM body shell including the radiator support panel, necessary so the XP front panels could be refitted. We also cut the section out of the XP firewall where the brake master cylinder bolts because it is different between XM and XP models.

The van then went back into full-time service for several more years until the paint started to fade and rust spots started to appear in the usual spots in the bodywork. Time for another rebuild and this time some more updating in the driveline department.

The three speed manual gearbox was swapped out for a Toyota Supra five speed and the rear end replaced with an eight inch Ford item from an American Falcon/Mustang with 3.4:1 ratio centre. Previously we had updated the original XP commercial diff by replacing the 4.11:1 gears with 3.5:1 gears from a sedan to make it more drivable on long distances. The Supra five speed and eight inch diff combination behind the trusty old XA 200 six has proven to be an ideal combination. Just the fitting of the five speed overdrive gearbox added 100 kilometres to the petrol tank and yet it pulls fifth gear really well even when loaded.

This last rebuild of XP 1000 was completed in about 2002 and nothing has changed since, apart from fitting NC Fairlane bucket seats to replace yet another worn out ute bench. We don't use the van quite as much these days and it rarely carries the heavy loads we once punished it with, but it does still see regular duty as a service vehicle getting us to and from some of the events. Since the last rebuild it has done two trips to Perth and back and we took it to Darwin in 2019 for the Top End Rumble, so it still sees plenty of road miles.

Next came another XP, this time a hardtop that I purchased from an advertisement in the Melbourne "Age" newspaper. It was slightly damaged as it had been in a nose to tail traffic bingle that had bent the rear bumper and pushed in the rear panel a little. Similar damage had been suffered at the front

ABOVE: The Model A Tudor body was purchased while still in Swan Hill, but only built after the move to Castlemaine in 1973. Don't you just love the big white letter tyres now! Note the tunnel ram on the 396 big block Chevy engine – it didn't stay there long and was replaced with a low-rise aftermarket manifold with Holley carby for much better driveability.

MY HOT RODDING LIFE

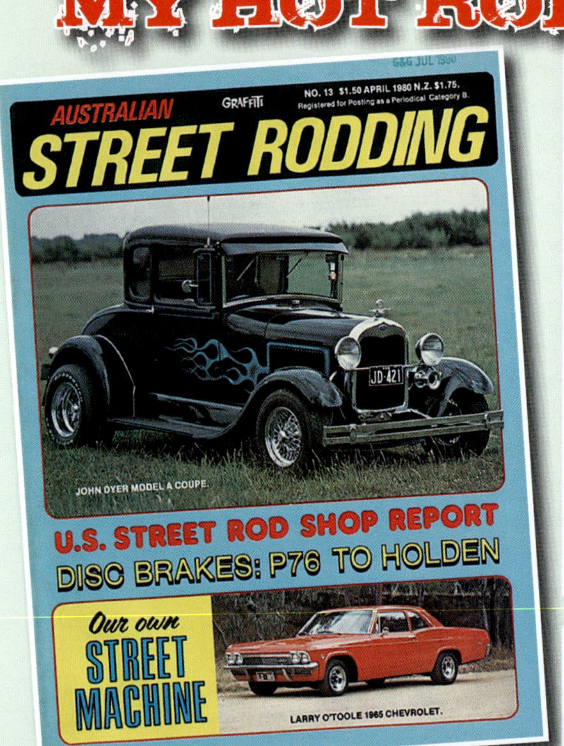

ABOVE & LEFT: The Chev has been lowered when the photo above was taken soon after the rebuild. Interior trim was done using woollen material from the local woollen mill in Castlemaine. At left it is shown on the cover of issue 13 of Australian Street Rodding magazine from April 1980, along with John Dyer's black with flames '28 Model A Ford coupe from Sydney.

ABOVE: Trio of Castlemaine Rods vehicles taken in the late 1970s. At left is Geoff Knape's Aussie bodied '34 Ford coupe, Bill Mussett's '36 Ford tourer, soon after its post-accident rebuild and change to orange paintwork and the Model A Tudor, still with its big, white letter tyres and high stance. Pinstriping was added to the Tudor shortly after this photo was taken and the tyres changed to radials all round that drastically improved handling and driveability. Bumpers were later removed and the undercarriage revamped to lower it substantially.

ABOVE: If this chopped '34 Ford ute looks familiar it is because it is the same one now owned by Clinton Horne. I started work by steeling it out and chopping the top and then sold it. Eventually it made its way to Clinton who completed it. The vehicle was damaged in an accident and awaits rebuilding.

RIGHT: In this photo the ute is basically as found in the bush near Maryborough, Victoria by Geoff Watts. We picked it up and deposited in my back yard where this photo was taken soon after.

where the bumper was bent and the nose of the bonnet thumped downward. The owner told me it was a good car but the brakes were bad – the supposed cause of the accident. It was drivable, so I drove it home to Castlemaine – carefully – as the brakes truly were bad, but I had a feeling all was not quite as it should have been. On getting it home I pulled the drums off to have a look at the brakes to find they were all brand new, they just hadn't been properly adjusted after fitting. That was soon rectified and we used the hardtop as a family car for several years thereafter.

When I bought this XP it was with the intention of building it up as a V8 powered version when the chance arose. A V8 XW Falcon wagon that I was able to buy locally proved the ideal donor car, so it came apart and the mechanicals (302 Windsor and C4 transmission) were transferred into the XP. The engine wasn't great, so it came back out for a quickie recondition and the entire car was refurbished from end to end and painted Monza Red with gold pearl overlay. This was a nippy little car in this form, but did have an overheating problem on very long distance drives on hot days that I never did fully cure. After several years as family transport I sold the XP Hardtop to champion bicycle racer, Bayden Cooke who kept it for some time, had some more work done on it and then sold it on again. Last I heard the car had been shipped to New Zealand.

While building the V8 XP we produced the simple book "How to Build Your Own Custom Street Car", based on this car and the V8 kits that Rod Hadfield's Castlemaine Rod Shop produced for early Holdens. The book sold like hot cakes, so much so that we reprinted it and sold most of the second print run too. In fact this simple, basic how-to book still sells well to this day.

When I built the V8 XP it was finished just a couple of weeks before it became compulsory for such cars to have an engineer's report prior to registration. That came into play in July 1988, about the time I started work on the 1930 Model A pickup that was featured as a continuous tech series in ASR at the time.

The pickup was purchased as the basic parts of a cabin from Kelvin Waddington, essentially it was a cowl and back panel with two doors wired together to resemble a pickup cabin. Everything else required for the project was gathered from swap meets or custom made to suit. Mark Rye made most of the pickup bed, using a badly beaten up original item that I purchased for the purpose. Only a couple of the corner brackets and the fender mounting brackets from that original bed were used, the rest was all made by hand by Mark, including perfect reproduction factory style rivets. The fenders, grille shell, valance panels and bonnet all came from swap meets, the fenders given a rebuild by Mark Rye as well, including removing the fender well from one of them. It took about 18 months to track down a set of fenders in any condition and I was starting to think I would never find any.

Running gear for the pickup consists of a 231 V6 Buick engine that came out of an Oldsmobile that was imported by Chev Offroad & Marine Engines. It had a Turbo 350 transmission attached that I had reconditioned and retained. The engine ran okay, so it was fitted as purchased and the project completed by 1990. The rear end is Compact Fairlane with my own custom made four link locating system and Torana XU-1 springs, front end is a Super Bell tube axle with XT Falcon solid disc brakes and a CAV four bar locating system.

At the time I had Rick Ling supply and fit one of the first custom wiring loom kits to the pickup in his Melbourne bayside workshop. It basically had everything you would expect in a modern car of the era, including four way hazard flashers, brake failure warning light, retractable lap-sash seat belts and even reversing lights. At the time of completion it was probably one of the most advanced street rods of the period for compliance with the regulations that we have now come to expect as normal. It too, still sees regular uses and has racked up many miles over the past 30 years, including a trip to Perth and back in 1994 for the first Sandgroper Nationals. Nine year old Allister was my passenger for that trip, I'm sure he still remembers how much fun we had, even though it was a very long way for a nine year old.

ABOVE: On my second trip to the USA in 1987 I stayed with Brian Bauer who mentioned he was interested in painting flames on his '30 Model A Tudor. I offered to do them on the spot, he agreed and the next day they were done! He still drives the car regularly and the flames are still there too.

Another XP van came into my life when we bought Supercar magazine to save it from being shut down altogether. This van was purchased out of Tasmania and driven up to us by friend, Hugh Nally from Hobart on one of his many visits to the mainland. We felt we needed a project vehicle for Supercar, but this time I wanted to do something really different. The plan was to chop the top on this otherwise pretty neat old Falcon and lower the suspension as much as possible, but still keep it legal. This was just after the original XP 1000 had been badly damaged by the Mercedes, so I reckoned we could tackle this top chop project using parts of both body shells. It is nearly always easier to chop a top if you have a spare roof from which you can take extra panels and minimize the amount of welding required.

To execute this big undertaking I made an extensive RHS frame to bolt inside the "Supervan" so that once I cut the roof off it everything would stay in alignment. Great care was taken and a lot of measuring done first in an effort to minimize any mismatches of body lines, door jambs etc. By cutting the roof off each van body in such a way that each section was cut slightly "over-centre" I was able to make it so that only one central weld was required right down the centre of the new roof. Being cut over-centre allowed for the difference that had to be made due to the slanted side panels moving outward as they came down two inches. All the measuring meant the join in the centre of the roof aligned almost perfectly. There was another trick at the

ABOVE: The freshly finshed pickup takes its place beside the Tudor that now wears pinstriping added with a Beugler striping tool. The pickup was registered in 1990 and has been on the road ever since.

LEFT: A very young Allister O'Toole pretends to be unloading sand from the pickup bed when we shot the finished feature photos for ASR magazine in our own back yard. Allister is now editor of Australian Street Rodding magazine, a position he has held for over 15 years – how time flies!

ABOVE: Rear shot of the pickup under construction shows the reproduction pickup bed made by Mark Rye. I bought a beaten up original bed from which he took dimensions and made an entirely new, perfect rendition. Only the tailgate hinges, fender mount brackets (not fitted here) and front stake pockets are original Model A items.

LEFT: The '30 Model A pickup project started out as just a cabin and doors and a stock chassis. This photo shows the completed rolling chassis with Buick V6 engine, Turbo 350 transmission and eight inch Ford rear end on Torana coil springs. Front end is four bar with dropped tube axle.

front of the roof to keep the windscreen and doors in alignment too. In order to make this easier a diagonal cut was made from the top of the windshield opening to the rear corner of the door on each side and the opposite halves of the two roofs were used to make this front section all good again. As a result there was only a small rectangular hole to be filled in the forward centre of the roof after the four sections were joined up again. I won't say it was an easy job, but the theory did match the eventual outcome quite well and it did all stay in alignment through the process.

The two inch chop was decided on so that we could use a hardtop windshield that still needed some modification at the outer corners as they are a squarer shape than the van windshield. Ray Charlton ground these corners to match the new opening and it fitted perfectly.

I planned to make a Street Boss 302 Ford engine for this project and did accumulate most of the parts required, but never did put it all together (I still have them all, so it could still happen). The engine bay was cleaned up extensively, edges finished and smoothed and joins welded up to make it much more attractive. I also went to quite a bit of trouble to fit a later model steering box, a swap that is more involved than it first appears, as the larger box needs to mount further forward in order to maintain correct steering geometry. That meant the right side suspension tower had to be modified for clearance and an early pitman arm broached to fit the spline on the later steering box.

To get the suspension down really low we looked at the possibility of fitting Castlemaine Rod Shop dropped Holden spindles into the Falcon front suspension. This took quite a lot of experimentation with steering arms and bump-steer checking, but we pulled it off admirably, ending up with virtually no bump-steer at all – a vast improvement over the stock Falcon system. Rod Hadfield then put this swap into production as a stock item. This single swap dropped the front ride height by three inches but retained full suspension travel.

At the rear end I cut out the rear wheel wells, widened them and moved their inner edges into the sub frame rail so they would take a 10 inch wide tyre. This meant the springs had to be moved inboard as well, so they were moved to inside the subframe rail and instead of using the Falcon springs that have a large rubber bush at the front, I used HK Holden springs that have a much smaller eye. That allowed the spring to be mounted 1-1/2 inches closer to the floor at the front. I had tacked together a new rear crossmember from which to mount the rear spring shackles, taking that end down a similar amount and had planned to fit deeper spring saddles on whatever rear end eventually goes into the vehicle. At that stage we ceased publication of Supercar to move Australian Street Rodding up to monthly publication, so the project was shelved. I still have it and fully intend that it will see the light of day some time in the future. As it sat when work ceased, the top of the roof was not much more than waist high, but it did still have full suspension travel at front and rear.

Some time in the 1980s I attended the Sultans Swap Meet when it was held on a Saturday instead of the normal Sunday and in a new location at a drive-in theatre. As a result there wasn't much of a crowd in attendance. As I walked in I was asked to make an offer on a '36 Ford Tudor body on a rolling chassis. Asking price was about $3750.00 from what I recall, but I wasn't looking for a '36 Ford, so passed it up and continued around the swap meet. When it came time to leave, the owner, Geoff Chowne from NSW asked me again if I would like to make an offer on the '36. He said he had brought it down from NSW and didn't want to cart it all the way back again. I said I would make him a silly offer of $1800.00 that he declined, but he came back with, "Make it $2000.00 and I will deliver it."

The deal was done on the spot and by mid-afternoon the '36 Tudor was unloaded in my backyard. It was pushed into the shed and there it stayed for nearly 25 years. Over all those years I collected parts, knowing I would build it one day. As it came, there was only the body with inside window trims on a rolling chassis that had the usual rust in it for this era vehicle. Gradually I accumulated all the missing parts and eventually decided it was time to make a start. When removed from its storage home, I found I had accumulated all the necessary body panels, some in multiples, but I was missing the cowl door. I found one at the next swap meet!

The total build of the '36 was extensively covered in Australian Street Rodding magazine over its too-long, 10 year build period. Having a heart attack halfway through the project certainly slowed things down, but the '36 has now been on the road since early 2017 and has covered over 20,000 kilometres. It was built for doing the long distance rod runs that have become common for us with all the comforts built in and an engine/transmission combination that suits the purpose perfectly. The 302 Windsor/BTR four speed auto running gear came from a '91 NC Fairlane, but has been extensively rebuilt and reconfigured to run sequentially injected LPG only. Using the LPG and having the four speed transmission makes the vehicle very economical to drive those long distances, yet it has ample power and is very comfortable to travel in. Front suspension is Mitsubishi L300

ABOVE: My many visits to the USA led to a long friendship with Tex Smith and we travelled many miles together going to Bonneville races, Goodguys West Coast Nationals etc. Through this association with Tex I got to meet and become friends with many legends of hot rodding in the USA. In this photo from Bonneville we are sharing the fun with Rod and Carol Hadfield.

MY HOT RODDING LIFE

ABOVE: This was how the XP 1000 project looked when we purchased it in about 1980. Although it looked tatty, the body was better than we thought once it was cleaned up and work began.

BELOW: After the second rebuild the van was used every day for many years by which time it was getting down again, as you can see in this photo. The paint had gone chalky and rust was becoming apparent in several places, so a third rebuild was undertaken in 2000.

ABOVE: The side windows were filled in with sheet metal and the body repaired where necessary before it was painted in my back yard. The colour chosen was Mazda Space Yellow. It is still the same colour today, but was changed to two pack at the last rebuild.

BELOW: The third rebuild was comprehensive with stripping to bare metal and professional bodywork and paint completed by good friend from Swan Hill days, the late Barry Fletcher and his son, Craig.

BELOW: XP 1000 has now been on the road for nearly 40 years and has provided excellent service in that time. About four years ago the lower body and sills had more rust repair work carried out. Engine is still the 200 XA Falcon six that we swapped in back in 1981, but now with Supra five speed transmission, XY front brakes, eight inch Ford rear end and Dragway wheels.

ABOVE: The red XP Falcon hardtop was purchased as a run down and slightly accident damaged original and rebuilt with donor V8 Windsor running gear from an XW wagon. The rebuild formed a large proportion of the content of the highly successful book How To Build Your Own Custom Street Car.

fitted with Holden stub axles, Commodore manual steering and HZ Holden disc brakes, while at the rear is a complete V8 VB Commodore rear end with its stock trailing arms and coil springs. The car is a delight to drive.

Salted away for a rainy day are a pair of small Fords that I purchased many years ago and were originally intended to be projects for my two older daughters when they obtained their driving licences. Well, they have had their driving licences for a very long time and the cars are still waiting. However, both are stored under cover so they aren't deteriorating any further. There is still hope for them to go back on the street one day. One is a '50-'51 Anglia ute, the other a panel van from the same era. It is interesting to note that the Anglia is top of the range for the era so it has wind-up windows, quarter windows, stainless steel trim and a full complement of gauges in the fancy bakelite dash. The van is the opposite, the absolute basic model with sliding glass in the windows, a single gauge in the simple steel dash panel and all painted finish with no polished or chromed trim at all. Both are quite complete but in need of full restoration/rebuild.

Now we have almost come full circle as my latest project is the Model A Bucket re-creation that is loosely based on my first hot rod. I sold the original car in 1975 and it went through several owners, was changed considerably and seems to have disappeared off the scene, although I last heard of it being in Canberra. That original car used the cowl and doors off the original Model A from the farm and the rear of the body was made using rear tourer doors and sheet metal to fill in the tapered shape at the rear as described at the start of this article. This time around I am making it a proper abbreviated roadster pickup body, but the finished car will wear the same combination of metalflake paint as used on the last iteration of the original when I owned it.

Parts for this one came from swap meets – the cowl and repro cab sections, doors from friends and acquaintances and the short bed I made myself in the home workshop. The chassis I purchased about 40 years ago at a Fridge Swap Meet in Ballarat, another of those "I don't want to take it home so make me an offer" purchases. It wasn't in great condition, but quite suitable for this project as I knew I would be cutting it up to suit. The engine is the 327 that was removed from the '65 Chevy, mated to a five speed T5 manual transmission that I bought locally with another eight inch Ford rear end, this one with a 3.5:1 ratio centre that I bought separately. Front end is a '32 Ford I-beam axle dropped by Garry Page, located by So-Cal hairpin radius rods and fitted with XY Falcon disc brakes and Commodore calipers. The rear suspension uses another of my home-cobbled four link systems (they are cheap and work very well) with stock six cylinder LJ Torana coil springs.

The bucket re-creation is my "retirement" project that I work on almost every morning for a couple of hours before going into the office to oversee the publishing operations. I must say I am thoroughly enjoying this early morning working time as it gives me a chance to lose myself, away from the cares of the world and just concentrate on making another hot rod. My "Hot Rodder Forever" switch is definitely in the jammed on position!

No regrets.

ABOVE: In the late 1990s the Model A Tudor chassis was given a quick makeover to lower it and provide more rear end clearance, plus fit dropped stubs to the front end. It was also converted to run straight LPG at the same time. The Tudor was back on the road in three months.

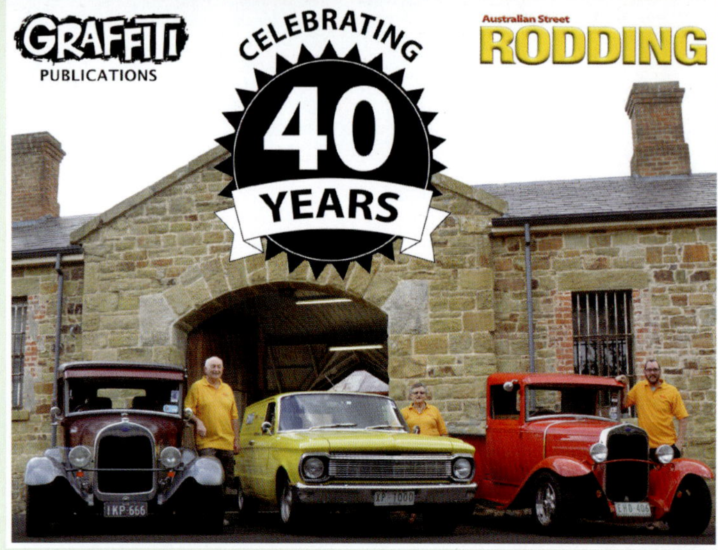

ABOVE: Photo shoot in front of the Old Castlemaine Gaol to celebrate the 40th Anniversary of Australian Steet Rodding magazine in 2017.

ABOVE & BELOW: The sad remains of the original XP 1000 bodyshell after it was seriously damaged by a wayward Mercedes. Parts of the roof were salvaged for the top chop on the Supercar magazine Supervan (above right) that is still not finished. The photo at bottom left shows how the two rooves were used to make one new roof with only one join down the middle by cutting each quarter slightly oversize to compensate for the taper in the side panels. Below left I am hammering on the weld while the late Harry Wright holds the dolly on the other side.

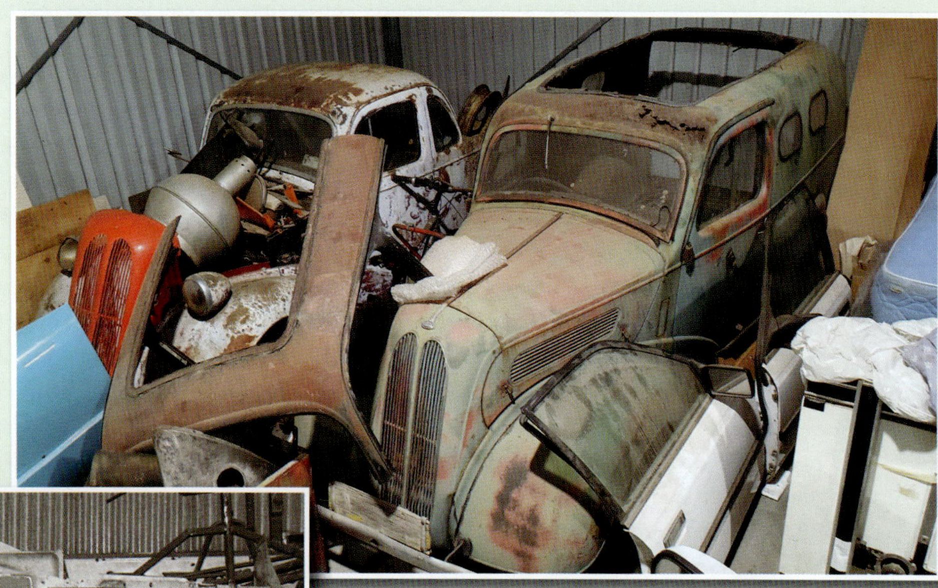

ABOVE: A soft spot for early Anglias led to the purchase of these two examples, an Anglia ute and a Fordson van that were to be project cars for our two daughters before they obtained their driving licences. Both girls are now in their mid-forties and the little Fords still wait. They are stored in dry conditions and I do have all parts to make them good again.

www.graffitipub.com.au

BELOW: The project '36 Ford Tudor took 10 years to complete, delayed mid-build by a heart attack and long recovery, but has now been in service since 2017. It runs 302 Ford Windsor on injected LPG with four speed auto, coil sprung Commodore rear end and Mitsubishi L300 front end with HZ Holden brakes.

ABOVE: The body shell was purchased on a rolling chassis at a Sultans Swap Meet at the Preston Drive-In Theatre in the 1980s. All other parts were purchased from swap meets over the next 25 years before work started on the project that appeared in an extensive how-to series in Australian Street Rodding magazine.

ABOVE & BELOW: Life goes full circle and I am now re-creating my first Model A Ford bucket in slightly different form as shown here. Essentially being put together from left-over parts, it uses an original cowl and doors, repro rear cab sections and a home made short pickup bed. Engine is 327 Chevy with fuellie heads that was in the '65 Chev when first rebuilt, T5 five speed manual transmission and eight inch Ford rear end. Front end is dropped '32 Ford I-beam axle with stainless steel hairpin radius rods. Seats are cut-down Toyota Camry buckets that will utilise a heavy roll across the back of the cab area as their top sections. Headers are home made with bypass pipes that take the exhaust inboard of the chassis in front of the firewall and through 2-1/4 inch pipes and mufflers to the back of the car. Wheels are original Magnums — 10x15 on the rear and 6x15 on the front in keeping with the late sixties/early seventies style of the bucket. Paint will be the same as the original bucket — Apricot Marigold and Chartreuse metalflake with ghosted lace pattern.

gallery

Charlie Smith
Lenexa, Kansas, USA

ABOVE: 1940 MERCURY FADE-A-WAY – A modern interpretation of the Matranga Merc Classic. This was originally done in blue and first shown at the S.E.M.A. Show's Concept Center in 1990. On the wall just above my primered street rod model.

It was rendered with mechanical pencil, pen and ink, markers, colored pencil and white-out correction fluid – using both sides on translucent paper. Then it was cut out and pasted to colored illustration board that had some air brush and oil stick colors applied.

Later by request, and with the use of the computer, the color was changed and the padded top and whitewall were added.

(The beautiful presentation lady... my wife of over 54 years.)

1949 Cadillac Eldorado

ABOVE: 1949 CADILLAC ELDORADO – Of course an Eldorado like this never occurred. I tried to do this one as if it was a GM Concept Car… sort of their answer to Ford's Continental. Hence, the use of the European (Continental) background. This was rendered entirely by computer using a low resolution starter image from the internet. Considerable work just to bring a low resolution 72 ppi image up to the size I work at, which is 18" x 12" x 300 ppi. Like all concept cars, I tried to include styling "tidbits" that would later find their way to other GM products - like the larger "dagmar" bumpers, the hooded headlights and the use of stainless trim (or aluminum) for the full fender skirts. Other subtleties like a change in wheel covers, enlarged taillights and a mild top chop (hardtop convertible) would show the way for many of GM's future offerings – as I imagined.

I spent my youth in a black leather jacket and my school days reading rod and custom magazines. Inspired initially from a "little book" article about Von Dutch, I was soon on an artistic roll. Before even gaining a driver's license, I was pinstriping, painting and lettering hot rods and race cars for more than just cigarette money.

I learned to weld in an uncle's fabrication shop and it wasn't long until I was customizing my own cars. That led to working in a custom body shop while still in my teens, with a wealth of tools (and new possibilities) at my disposal.

From an early age I had always liked to draw; especially anything with wheels. While working in an active body shop I soon realized I couldn't build all the ideas I had floating around in my head. I turned back to drawing as a faster and "at hand" way of fulfilling my automotive and creative dreams. Been with the "at hand" method ever since. Seems to be working.

While my artistic interests have always been varied, I moved on to where "making a living" was most readily available. Eventually running my own Illustration and Graphic Arts business. This, in turn, led to book and magazine illustration, science-fiction art, logos and graphics for a number of clients as well as steady work from advertising agencies. Drawing "cars" was still, always planted firmly in the back of my mind throughout.

A chance encounter with a "silk screen" project led to some wonderful new opportunities. It seems I had a knack for creating colorful silk screen images, which then led to the production of an entire line of related sportswear. Wasn't long until the emphasis focused on the automotive portion of the "offering" and that finally led me back to my roots in the early '80s… "the rod and custom scene".

Travelling the Rod and Custom "Car Show" circuit, offered me an appreciative group of buyers for my product, as well as exposure to all the "movers and shakers" in the industry… and too, all the major Rod and Custom publications. Wasn't long, until I was right where I'd always wanted to be; designing all those things with wheels! And it seemed, to still be working.

On an influential note: I found inspiration from my Grandfather who gave me my first lettering and pinstriping brushes as well as local Kansas City auto artist – Tom Davison. Then via the "little books" from Kenny Howard (Von Dutch) and regular auto design contributors like Larry Evans and Tom Daniel. Later, when it came to contemporary auto

BELOW & RIGHT: CHAZ NORM ART – I told Bob Reynolds of the NSRA once, that they should give Norm Grabowski the "Lifetime Achievement Award". If you look at early pictures when the Street Rod Association began, if it wasn't for "Fad Ts" there wouldn't have been much of a gathering to begin with. Of course Norm was instrumental in creating the look with the original Kookie Kar, and after Tommy Ivo dropped by to take measurements, the mold was cast for a lasting and unique category of the street rod culture.

If Andy Brizio was the "Rod Father", then Norm was definitely the "Rod God" without question.

Norm and I remained close friends from our first meeting in Oklahoma City, 1986 until his untimely passing just a few years back. We spent several Christmases celebrating at our home and did lots of car shows together… always a "crazy trip".

In 1990 at the Nats in Columbus - Ohio, Norm asked me about doing a character or some permanent image he could use as a "logo" or identifying mark. I took a couple of photos at the show, and in early 1991, I did drawing "Norm 1" as my first character study. Later that year, as invited guests of the St. Ignace Michigan Car Show (we went together) I did "Norm 2". I liked them both and later he was to use them on a couple of his vehicles as proof of "no doubt" ownership.

Anyway, that eventually led to "Norm 3" (a full body characterization). I liked it as well, but Norm complained that , "I look like a little prune". His physical presence and strength were big things to Norm, so "little prunes" was just not going to work.

Later, working towards a "logo" like image, I created "Norm 4". Although even I thought it to be a bit grotesque (I never showed it to Norm) it did however set the stage for what was to come.

I decided to quit thinking about character studies or realistic images. I decided to find the essence of Norm without any references. I taped a piece of blank typewriter paper to my drawing board and over time, as I passed by, I tried to find him with an added line or erasure. Took about two weeks and finally I was sure I'd captured him with "Norm 5". I called Norm and told him the task was finished… his only question was, "Do I have glasses on?" I said, "Yep, done deal", and then quickly added his spectacles to complete the logo and cover my tiny little lie. He was delighted with the results and even I don't know how I found him and actually made a cartoon recognizable to so many. Seems to have worked… I was just along for the ride.

All done with 2B pencil on typewriter paper.

1954 MERCEDES BENZ – This category features two modified versions of the same auto. The wheels and the matte black paint were the only inclusions requested by the client.

Both versions rendered entirely on the computer using "dirty reference shots", in a weedy area behind the client's place of business. The pavement and background were from a photo I took at an I-70 Turnpike Service-Stop near Topeka, Kansas.

ABOVE: M•B FEUERWAGEN – The "Fire Wagon" includes suicide rear doors, a chopped top, special bumpers and custom designed flames. Then a drop to the correct ride height and rolling on wheels as the client requested.

BELOW: M•B STRASSEROD – The "Street Rod" maintains the stock top height for a more formal "classic cruiser" look. It features the new wheels, suicide back door entry and custom bumpers. Its main modifications are its fade-a-way front fenders and the 300 SL gullwing side vents.

©2001

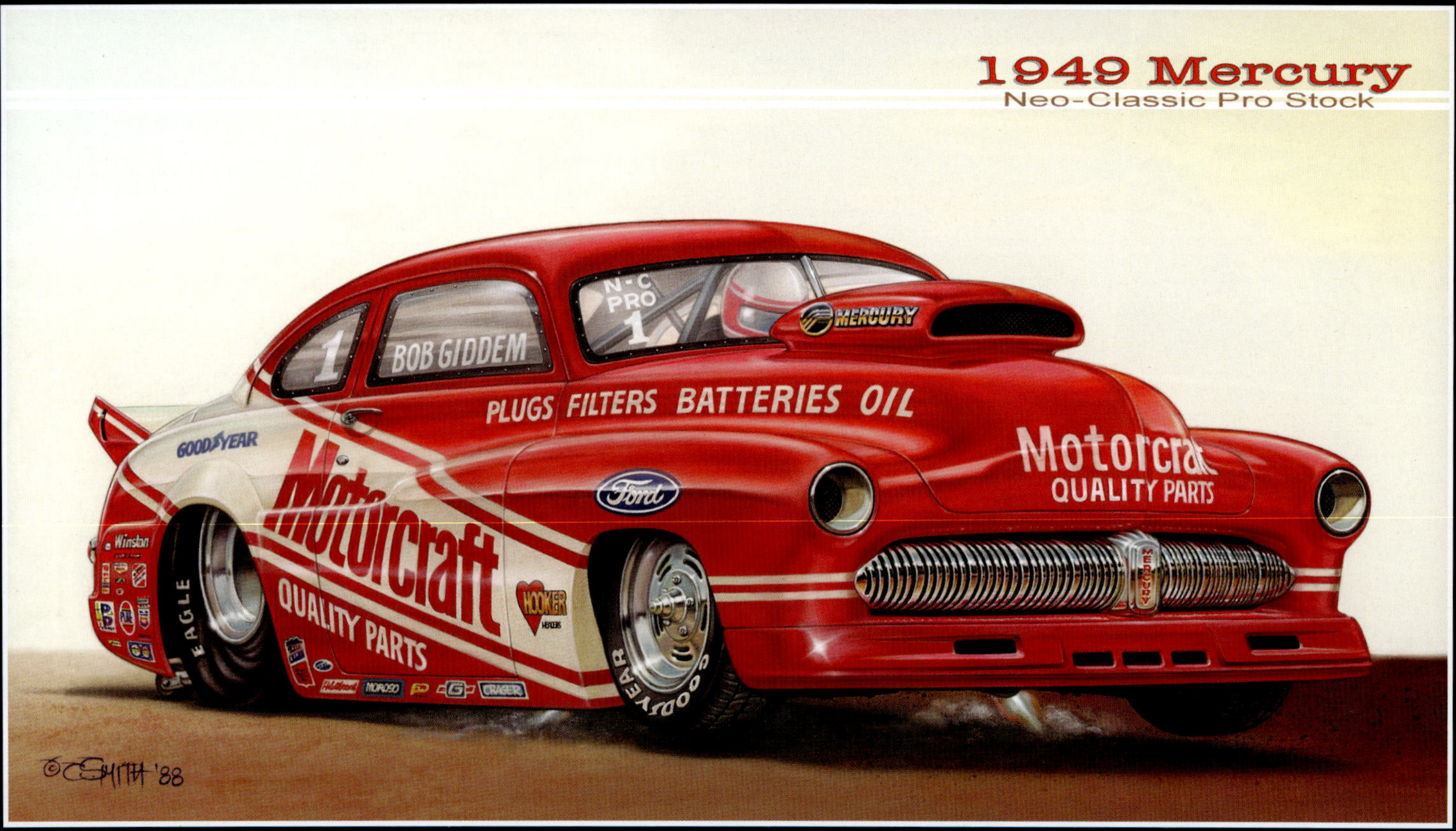

ABOVE 1949 MERCURY PRO-STOCK: This was the lead-off design for the Hot Rod Magazine article. "Future Thought" in January, 1989. The '49 Mercury Pro-Stock was proportioned (shortened and widened) to fit the dimensions of Bob Glidden's late model T-Birds. Even the front bumper had styling inlet features similar to some of the Motorcraft T-Birds at the time.

BELOW & OPPOSITE – STUDEBAKER VX GTP: This was an idea I've had rolling around in my mind for a long time. A '53 Studebaker styled "Grand Touring Prototype". It just seemed the perfect design to lend itself to a cab forward, rear engined auto design. Before doing the last of the finish "GTP" computer illustrations, I did these two preliminary color drawings of what I was proposing to do with this current illustration, also done in 2004.

ABOVE: SO-CAL STUDEBAKER PUSH-TRUCK – Pete Chapouris and I collaborated on several projects through the years, following our first job together... an eight color silk-screen design featuring his flamed purple '39-'40 Ford ragtop. This Stude pickup concept I originally did in 2009, as a nondescript design with an "artsy" graphic background. Later, in 2012 I did additional work on the computer and portrayed it in So-Cal colors as a "push-truck" at the Salt Flats, with all the necessary surroundings.

ABOVE '36 FORD CONVERTIBLE – FRONT VIEW: Features the traditional red wheels and grille. Also included are massive side pipes through open hood sides and '37 Ford headlights in custom pods.

ABOVE RIGHT '36 FORD CONVERTIBLE SIDE VIEW: From the '37 headlights through the chopped "Carson like" top and ending out back with the blue-dots… it's close to the epitome of a classic Ford roadster.

THE DANBURY MINT: I did many designs for Danbury, including specialty cars and general interest designs. This selection includes four designs that went into production – three rod and custom designs and one of general interest… a Model T delivery. (Page 30 - Top) The designs were all pencil, ink, marker, colored pencil and white-out on translucent paper (working both sides). No airbrush, except for the background board the designs were cut-out and pasted upon. Most of the designs were coordinated with a master model builder. Danbury required that parts (if possible) be pirated from their existing model offerings, so careful planning was important in any customizing process.

ABOVE '56 FORD F-100: This design was mildly changed from the original Danbury design. A new candy-tangerine paint job and Shop Truck signage was added to the door.

1936 Ford Custom

ABOVE: '35 FORD PICKUP – Includes a '37 Ford grille and hood with '41 Chevy pickup headlight pods and custom front nerfs. An upright side exhaust, Caddy caps and tonneau cover completed the overall classic look.

BELOW: DALE'S SKYLARK – This two view design features front and back illustrations - both done completely on the computer. They were digitally developed with a Raster program, then the two-tone paint was applied and finally striped with a Vector application. The wheels that I illustrated were a type requested by the client. Most of my illustrations, I actually feel like I'm building the car as I proceed to completion. It all has to work in reality... I don't like to be nebulous with the presentation... reality over "artsy" – always.

ABOVE: RAILWAY EXPRESS – '25 Ford T-Delivery is one of many special interest designs I did for Danbury. Complex and difficult to illustrate, but still always a favorite of mine.

LEFT: GREEN HORNET – With this particular design, I was able to more fully capture the sketch-like qualities I was after, while continuing through the coloring-in process.

BELOW: Here's the original sketch and the color rough, before going to the finish illustration.

TWO CHOPPER DESIGNS – When the superb hot rod designer Thom Taylor called me about a book he was doing (How to Draw Choppers Like a Pro) and asked for my contributions, I said, "certainly". I had done contributions to a couple of Thom's "How to Draw Cars" books before. But after hanging up, I had to seriously think about my effort, realizing I'd never really done a motorcycle design with any seriousness before.

You can see by the "Green Hornet" design above and the "Bad to the Bone" to follow that I resorted to "full bodied bikes" to cover some of my shortcomings over the mechanical aspects… not wanting to offer myself to ridicule from the Biker's World. I must have passed the audition, because both my efforts became two page spreads when Thom's Chopper Book went to press.

I did these two designs in sort of an old world – new world way. Wanting to keep a sketch-like quality to the illustrations. I started with a pencil sketch, then scanned it to the computer and tried my best to keep the sketch qualities of the original through the coloring-in process. I think it worked pretty successfully… more so with the Green Hornet. As I go along, the illustration itself dictates the degree of "finish" in the final artwork… I'm just along for the ride!

Today, I'd probably be more capable of opening up my motorcycle designs for a more complete mechanical view. My youngest son builds "bikes" professionally and I've designed a couple for him. His knowledge wouldn't allow me a "nut or bolt" out of place, and he'd certainly give the "old man" the business for any visual misrepresentations. Besides, he loves to show the mechanical side of his "builds", not to cover it up.

ABOVE & LEFT: BAD TO THE BONE –
Here's the original front and back sketch. Using the rear view and final color by computer… utilizing both the old and new way of doing design work ~ with Lead and Silicon!

BIRDS AND CATS:

The focus of all these designs came from two original illustrations (pictured in this introduction) that appeared in a January, 1989 article in Hot Rod

Magazine called "Future Thought". In this 1989 article I proposed (amongst others) these two contemporary custom designs utilizing 1983 to 1988 Thunderbirds and Cougars as the basic element in building modern customs. I said in the article, "Why spend a lot of money swapping late model mechanicals and suspensions into an old car when you could customize a late-model car". Even truer today, since these models in pretty good shape are still available for relatively very little dinero and... think of the improved "ride quality".

The "shoebox like" design at top from the Hot Rod article, is built from a big window 1987-'88 Thunderbird. The design at right uses a 1983-'86 Cougar as its starting point.

From the beginning, I always tried to utilize most all the sheet metal and glass from the base models – just cosmetic changes. One styling constant that remained with all designs was raising the side window sills so that there was a continuous flow from rear quarter, through the door, and continuing through the upper profile of the front fender. As well, these and the four designs that followed, also have about a two or three inch extension on the front fender wheel flair to help with the lowered car's turning clearance.

All the designs were rendered the old fashioned way. The original Hot Rod article designs were marker on illustration board. The four later designs utilized semi-transparent paper while working color on both sides of that material. Working both sides allows for smooth transitions of color, both pencils and markers and very little air brush (if any). I used mechanical pencil, rapidiograph for precise black ink, marker, colored pencil and white-out correction fluid for "hot spots". The backgrounds of the later designs were smeared on the backside with oil sticks and highlighted with colored pencil on the front.

BELOW: GREEN COUGAR – "Green with Envy" is built from a 1983 to 1986 Mercury Cougar, from the rear it definitely has the features of the 1952 to 1953 Mercury custom. See the deck lid that still maintains the stock Cougar raised sculptural features.

ABOVE: BURNT BIRD – "Modern Matranga" is built from a big back window 1987 to 1988 Ford Thunderbird. Sort of has the same amount of work that went into the Matranga and Hirohata Mercury and this design was influenced by both.

LEFT: BLUE COUGAR – "See Cruise" is built from a 1983 to 1986 Mercury Cougar. It has the look associated with a 1953 Mercury custom. A porthole and graphic Buick like side sweep completes the classic look.

BELOW: PURPLE T-BIRD – "Purple Reign" The most production-like of the four, this one would be built from a 1983 to 1986 Thunderbird. Extensive work to the rear quarters and front extension, but still easy to see the stock T-Bird that it was.

LONG AGO, with the exception of the Chevy Crew Cab, these designs first appeared in a Hot Rod magazine article called "The Future" - January, 1988. The following year saw the Crew Cab, the '49 Mercury Pro-Stock (page 26, top left) and several other of my designs appear in a followup article called "Future Thought" – January, 1989. This later article also led to the future development of the "Birds and Cats" designs shown previously on pages 32 and 33 of this Gallery.

ABOVE: '55 CHEVY CREW CAB – In the U.S., so many old four door Tri-Fives are still rusting in the fields, because no one seems to want them. What a waste of precious metal. They could become great starter cars if only a new purpose could be found. I therefore proposed this idea for all that previously unwanted rare steel. Make a crew cab pick-up out of them.

RIGHT: HOT ROD '50 MERCURY – This one wasn't your typical traditional Mercury custom... far from it! A lot of people thought it used a stock Camaro top from an actual production car, but I meant it to have a completely original top with specially formed back glass. Like Egon Necelis' 1941 Buick custom-rod to follow in this Gallery, it featured a removable front top portion and unique wheels.

LEFT: BACKWARDS '63-'64 CORVETTE – This one wasn't as readily apparent as the backwards Stude, but it follows the same "reversed body" theme. So yeah, maybe this wasn't what everyone was thinking when they looked at these Stingray body styles... but now that you've seen it turned front to back... tell me it doesn't work traveling in this direction – just as well.

ABOVE – HOT ROD ROADSTERS: It didn't take long for Hot Rod to telephone me about all the tires on the roadster designs. Just something I saw at S.E.M.A.... duals that were supposed to channel rainwater away from the car. Seemed like a good idea at the time, using them on a fenderless highboy. I told them I always thought that "highboys" had sort of a utilitarian beauty and I felt the dually tires were appropriate. Can't say I'm partial to the look now, but I'm still liking my body-work.

BELOW – BACKWARDS '50 STUDE: I'm probably not the first person who said these little missiles were going the wrong way. However saying is one thing... showing is another. Here 'tis, and it looks "right as rain" to me. Apparently others are in concurrence, as this design brought me lots of happy response from a wide variety of countries... even as far away as Australia and New Zealand.

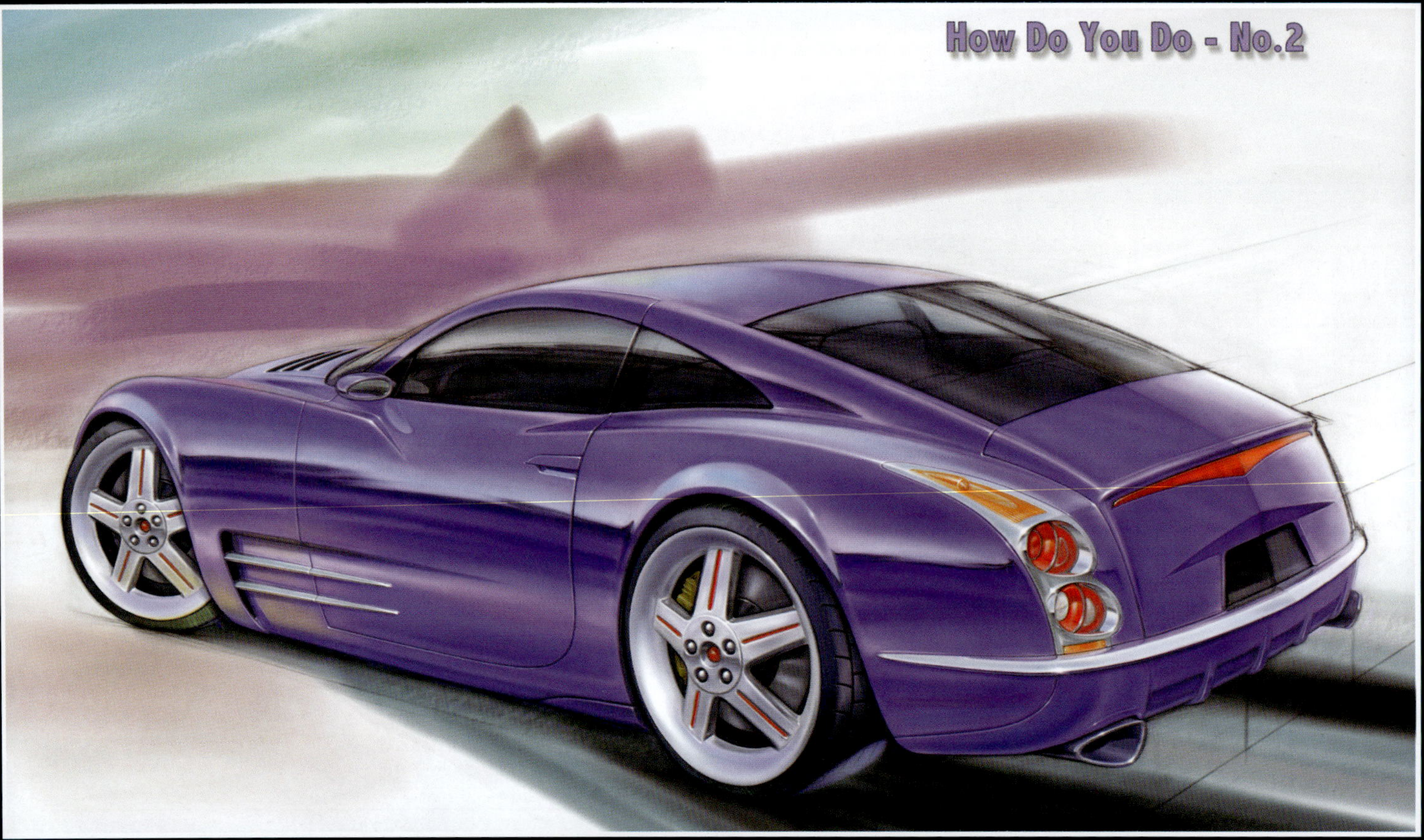

ABOVE: HOW DO YOU DO - NO. 2: – This was a "step by step" demonstration of how to illustrate cars by computer. It was a 12 part demonstration starting with a pencil sketch and proceeding to develop different details of refinement. That's why certain areas are to a high degree of finish, and yet other areas are still "sketch like" – like the rear of the car and the interior. This ran on the internet for several years and on more than one website… my own while it was then active.

Mercedes-Benz SRE McLaren

Pointing Stuttgart in a different Direction.

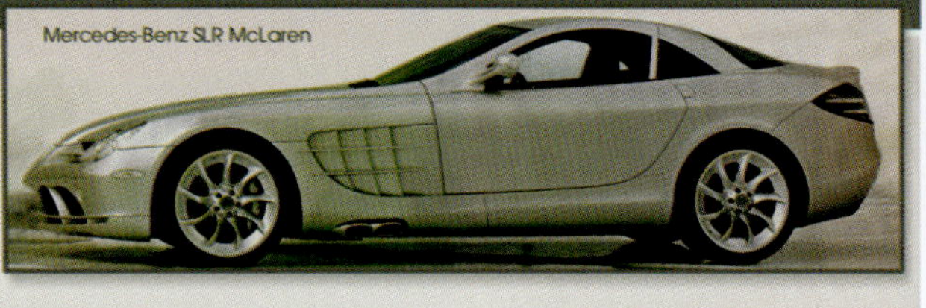

MCLAREN SRE (BEFORE AND AFTER): This exercise in manipulation of a low-rez product image derived from the internet, should show the degree I will go to when the design warrants an adjustment or complete revamp. This was nothing more than my personal endeavor to spin this "front engine" offering from a major manufacturer in another direction altogether. Hopefully I passed the audition with my aggressive, rear engine design. The "original" is in the upper right of this revamped illustration.

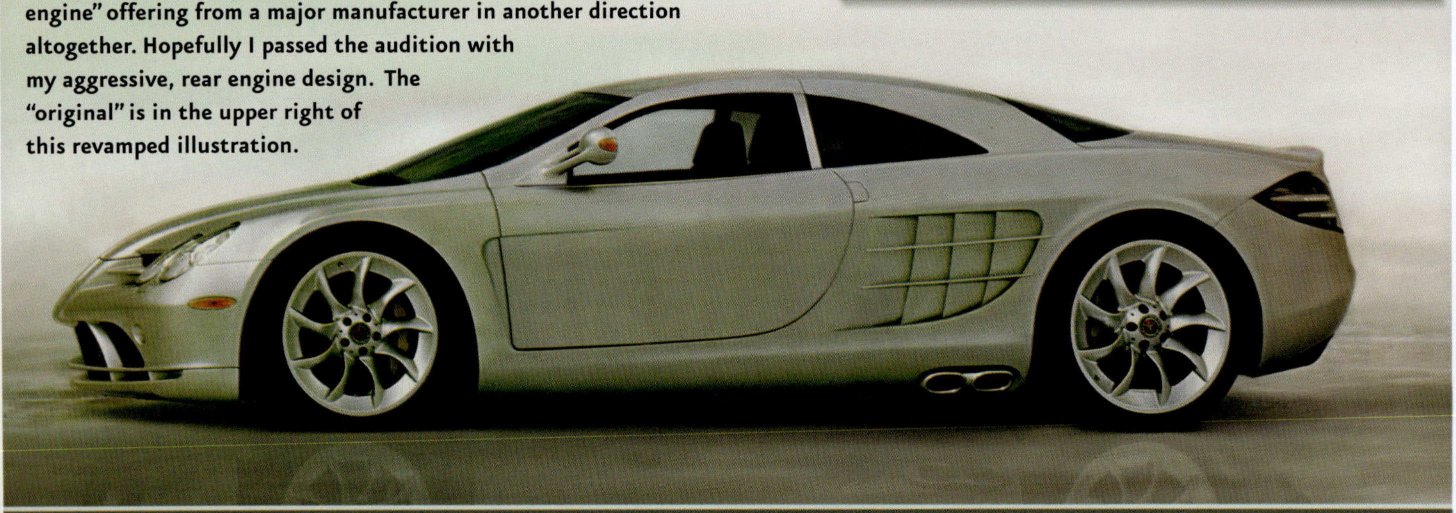

Rear-engine concept by C. Smith

ABOVE: EL CADMINO – After placing my grocery and flower hauler design next to a beautiful Frank Lloyd Wright synagogue, I sort of changed my perception of this styling effort. When first designing this Cadillac concept, I originally saw it as the perfect little ride for a busy woman, with lots of running and errands to do... albeit with plenty of "style points" to gather. However, I can also see ol' Frank, if his driver's license is still current, trading his custom Continental in on this and toting his drawings and architectural plans to one of his many building or home construction sites. For that matter, my wife and I might look pretty stylish in this "Caddy Hauler" as well.

BELOW: NEO BUICK – JOB 41: This was a contemporary design utilizing many of the styling features I incorporated in my original concept for Egon Necelis' 1941 Buick custom-rod. It was first presented in the Top Flite Designer's Gallery along with the debut of the '41 at the 1990 Street Rod Nationals in Columbus, Ohio. You might notice that this version's front fender, is actually a modified rear fender from a 1941 Buick or other GM offerings from the era. Turned back to front of course. The car would have its wonderful gas-guzzling engine mounted outback or amidships. Compare this design with my related design for Egon's Buick on the following pages.

ABOVE: EGON'S 1941 BUICK – In 1986, at the Street Rod Nationals in Oklahoma City, Egon Necelis asked me to design a '41 Buick "torpedo bodied" car for him.

In those days, and without the internet to correspond with, sometimes the construction process led things to get somewhat out of sequence in the process. Decisions would get "welded in" at times on the "builder's end" that made it almost impossible for the designer, to correct. Believe you me, there were hundreds of additional detail drawings exchanged in the process, not all arriving in time for a "fix". Never-the-less, the final results were about as close as I could have hoped for at the time... working 1500 miles away from each other and just taking a look "first hand" once a year.

I'll try to show pictorially the process from beginning to end, and then finally summarize what the above 2002 post-build Illustration is all about. Of course it was the '80s, so any initial illustrated material sent to Egon was done the old fashioned way; pencil, ink, and marker.

HERE'S THE STARTER CAR AT EGON'S SHOP (at left) – Then a couple of "build references" (at top right) that Egon always had hanging on the shop wall near the car's construction. This version was called "The Centurion". One thing of special note; I always meant for the body to be shortened at least six inches behind the door's back cut line – didn't happen! When the first build pictures arrived, the body was already firmly attached to a '72 Buick frame and the car's length already permanently established.

Also included with the first designs was an alternative... a car that Egon was building at the time of his unfortunate demise in 1997 – I called that design the "Riviera Classic" (previous page, bottom right).
THEN A FEW PICTURES AS CONSTRUCTION BEGAN IN JANUARY 1987 – As he followed my exterior illustrations, I subsequently sent Egon designs for special components and features. These included renderings for the wheels, engine compartment and then lastly... a completely integrated interior.

This wheel design from early 1988, we were to adapt from, as time and tire sizes evolved. We finally settled on 16" front and 17" for the rear. The big "machined wheels" were a cutting edge idea at the time and eventually won "Product of the Year" at the NSRA Nationals. Next in line was an idea for the engine compartment (mid 1988). As far as I know, the first "engine shroud cover" for a street rod, or even a production car for that matter.
AND FINALLY, A COMPARISON BETWEEN A STOCK '41 BUICK AND EGON'S FINAL ACCOMPLISHMENT – FINISHED IN JANUARY, 1990 (see bottom picture here and page 41) – Now, about that 2002 Computer illustration at the top of Page 38. It wasn't until after Egon's passing that I decided to illustrate the Buick the way I would have liked to have seen the finished product.

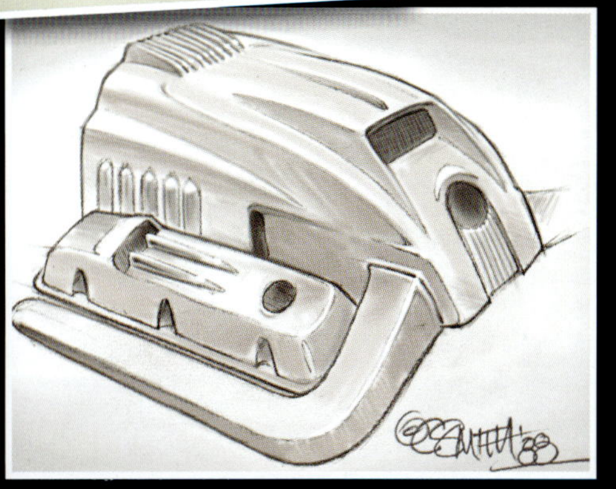

The shortened body, softened side window surrounds and more crown to the top were just a few of the subtle modifications this illustration depicts. Different shapes to both front and back fenders as well as the correct placement of the grille and taillight struts, get the car looking just the way I would have liked it.

The car was rendered entirely with digital tools, including the wheels. The woodland background is generated from a small narrow picture copied from a "book jacket" – then repeated several times at different elevations to accomplish the overall scene.

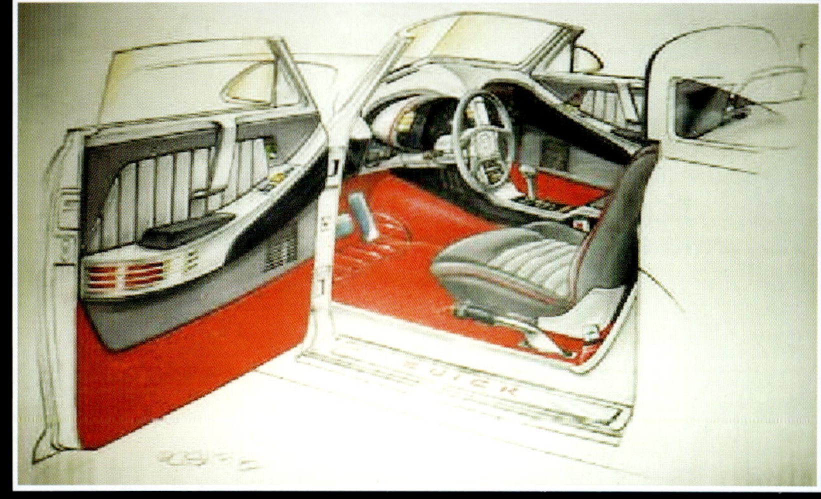

EGON'S 1950 MERCURY – Sometime during the course of building the red '41 Buick, Egon asked me to design him something different using a 1950 Mercury he had acquired recently. It was my understanding at the time, that the car eventually would be for youngest son, Egon Jr – who now worked at the body shop with his father.

So, armed with several new designs I met Egon in Columbus, Ohio for the 1987 Street Rod Nationals. It was also at this show, hearing about my new designs for a '49-'50 Mercury, that Philippe Danh and Pat Ganahl of Hot Rod Magazine inquired if they could have a look. After viewing, they asked if I'd like to contribute designs to a Hot Rod article on "The Future", coming up in their January 1988 issue. Of course, this was an opportunity I couldn't say no to, and I jumped at the chance... doh!

Anyway, Egon and I settled on a front design titled 9/87 and it set the tone for the rest of the car's styling... which would follow over the course of the next year or so. I believe that Egon began construction on the Mercury, sometime in late 1990 or early '91.

MERC 987 FRONT (OPPOSITE PAGE TOP) - This 2002 after-the-build illustration depicts the Mercury as I would have liked to see it finished. Egon came close to my design renderings but, it had been mounted on a late model chassis like the Buick, and it never did have the right "ride height" for my taste. I also adjusted the top's crown and gave a more graceful slope to the side window's outline, along with many other minor adjustments. It was all rendered on the computer with digital tools. The roadway and background were from a photo I took in the Missouri Ozarks... somewhere along MO-5 highway as I stopped to do my "bizness".

MERC 987 REAR (OPPOSITE PAGE CENTER) – This composite photo-like composition was made from artwork and low resolution images and meant to depict something that never happened... all three of the cars I designed for Egon in one setting. I tried to depict the texture and atmosphere of an actual photo, while recreating the Shop as it appeared in the early '90s. It no longer looks as such, since Egon Jr. has taken over and completely revamped the operation from his

Dad's time there. The old "quonset hut" main building is now totally engulfed in a new and much larger structure. As a starting point I used an old photo sent by Egon long ago, to show me how close he'd come to my designs for the back recessed window and other taillight and rear panel details.

Then the actual recessed rear window and rear quarter designs that he followed for direction... center exhaust from the red design, the rest from the yellow:

Then next to Egon in this "detail picture" (as he washes the red Buick with hose and water bucket) is the other '41 Buick design (The Riviera Classic) parked next to the outside wall of the shop. Egon was actually working on this design at the time of his passing. Surprisingly, this unfinished car showed up "out of the blue" at the Street Rod Nationals in 2010.

MERC CONCEPT 90 (ABOVE TOP) – This optional design illustration was presented to Egon at St. Ignace, Michigan in 1991. The Mercury had started out as a two door post design, but after seeing in-progress pictures of the "top chop with post", I was trying to guide the project to a more graceful "hardtop look". This never did become as graceful in execution as I would have liked, but a definite improvement over maintaining the original "B pillar". In doing this illustration, I took the opportunity of illustrating a more traditional version of the frontal styling as well, I don't remember that anyone ever mentioned the difference... or they (he) didn't want to think about any additional changes. Yeah I know – something all us "pencil pushers" are guilty of... always another change.

BONNEVILLE SPEED WEEK 2021

ABOVE: Looks like it was a disappointing year for the 556 Roadster, they didn't figure in the results at all, indicating they didn't make a successful run.

ABOVE RIGHT: The American Speed Center Special spent Speed Week doing licensing passes and succeeded in reaching 169.177 mph in the process.

ABOVE & ABOVE RIGHT: The Bean Bandits have been racing for what seems like forever and this year campaigned the Birdrock Mobilgas Special D Gas Model A Ford roadster that went fastest at 163.450 mph.

BELOW: Wild looking BGCC CAL Auto Comp Coupe, of Ron Cizek is based on a '34 Chevy coupe body. The team made several runs for the week and ended up with a best speed of 279.176 mph on the long course.

Words: Larry O'Toole,
Photos: Les Winter

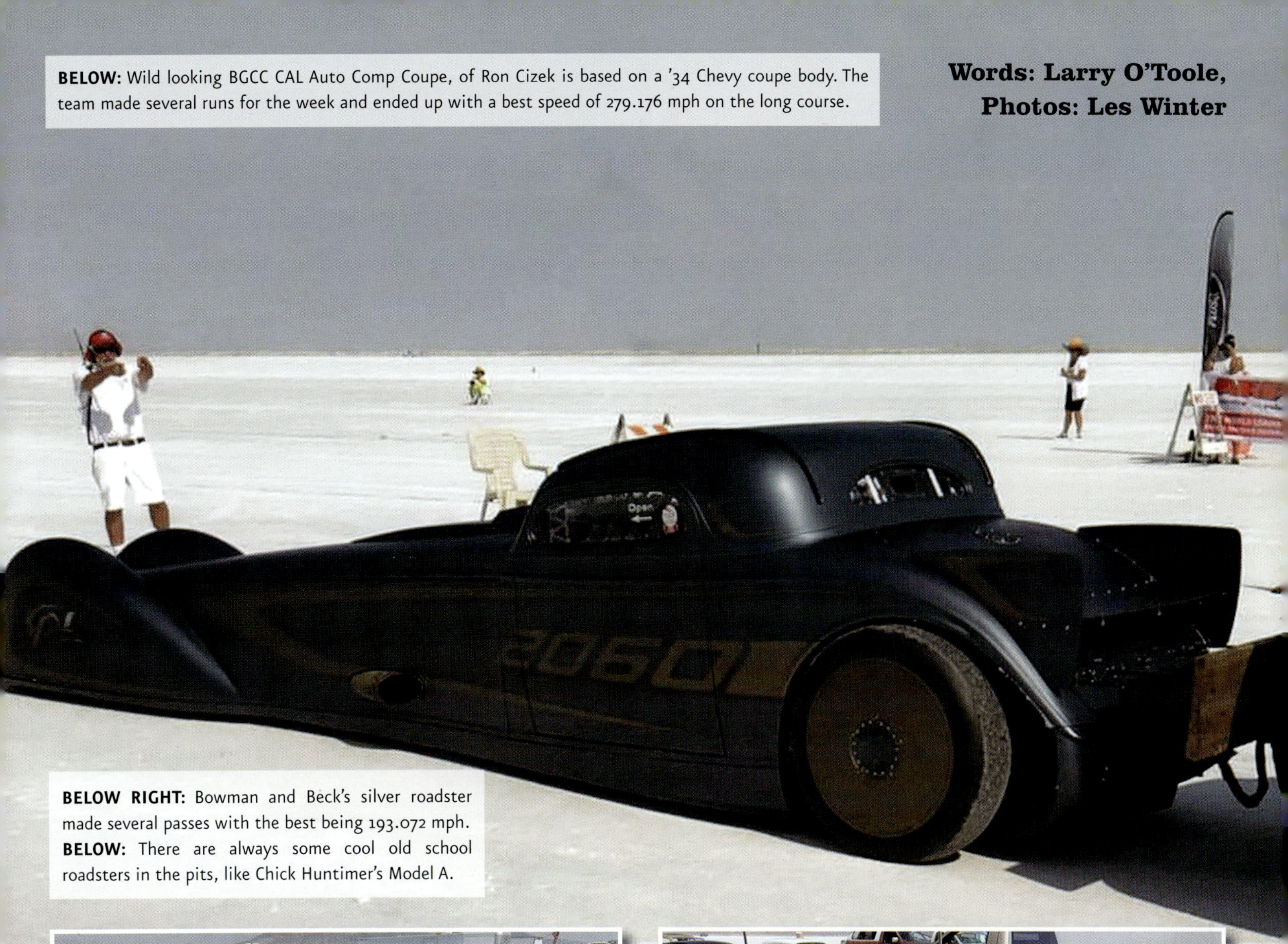

BELOW RIGHT: Bowman and Beck's silver roadster made several passes with the best being 193.072 mph.
BELOW: There are always some cool old school roadsters in the pits, like Chick Huntimer's Model A.

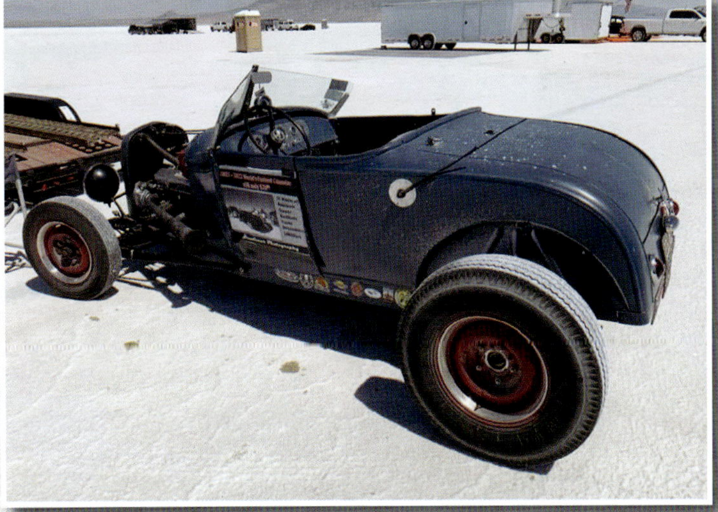

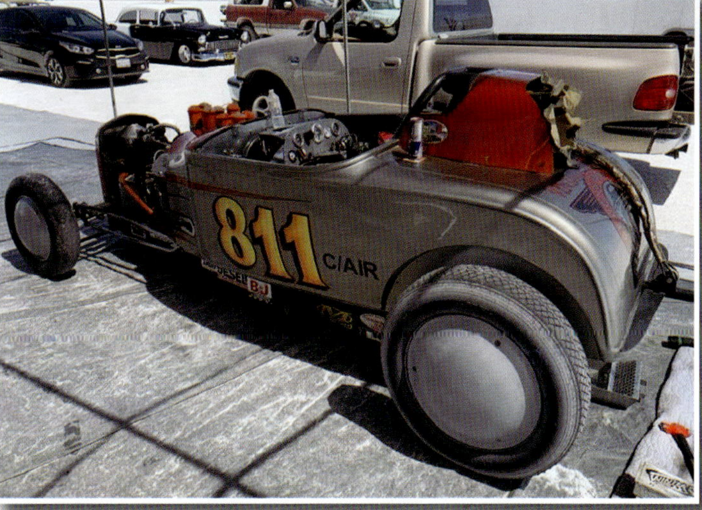

A visit to the Bonneville Salt Flats is something high on every hot rodders wish list. Expatriate Aussie, Les Winter has been living in Texas over the past several years and has been to Bonneville before. But COVID–19 convinced Les it was time for another Bonneville road trip while the possibility was available. Les and several of his Coil Busters club friends teamed up for the road trip to Wendover, Utah, the nearest habitation to the Bonneville salt flats, situated just a few miles away to the east of the town in Utah.

The township itself is divided, half of it in Utah and the other half in Nevada and the two halves are quite a contrast. The Utah side has motels and a few shops together with scattered housing tracts. On the Nevada side, where gambling is permitted, there are several casinos that dominate the skyline and provide Bonneville racers and visitors with respite from the hot desert climate.

Speed Week 2021, started off uncomfortably as strong winds buffetted the salt flats, sending awnings flying and tangling their frames. For that reason, racers are advised to remove all such awnings each evening as the wind can sometimes spring up unannounced during the night. The hot dry summer experienced in the western states of the USA also resulted in smoke-filled hazy skies and even floating ash that deposited itself on the salt flats. Nearly 500 race teams entered this year, all keen to make their best runs yet.

The smoky atmosphere cleared somewhat by the time racing

ABOVE: Maybe the ideal transport for sauntering around on the salt – a garage-find 1930 Model A closed cab pickup.

ABOVE RIGHT: Or if you like it a little more stylish, how about a two tone '30 Model A coupe with steel wheels, Deuce truck grille and radically dropped headlight bar.

RIGHT: All hands on deck to push this classy looking Deuce roadster up to the start line. Eight In A Row Racing went a stout 175.440 mph in the vintage engine XO/BFR class.

BELOW: Fun on the salt for all these hot rodders lined up for a picture for the folks back home. It's almost standard procedure for non-racing visitors at Speed Week.

BELOW: The Wimer & Darien team suffered a spin on their first run but then went 201.673 mph on the long course.

BELOW: The X/GR roadster of the Corl Competition team ran consistently during the week and posted a fastest speed of 142.976 mph.

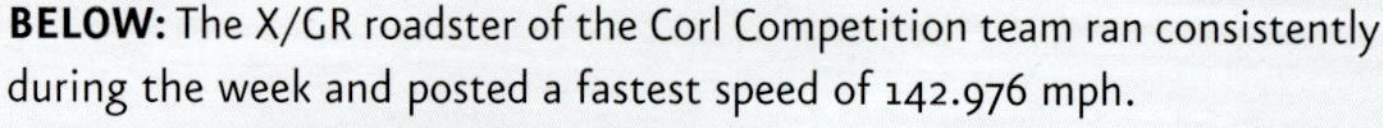

ABOVE: The Noice/Confal B/STR Model A Ford ran strong at 209.611 mph, but only made one run for the week. Back on the trailer in the pits indicates there might have been a problem continuing.

ABOVE LEFT: Marino-Batto's scalloped Deuce roadster also performed admirably with a vintage engine, running a best speed of 167.205 mph.

LEFT: Our correspondent, Les Winter is an expatriate Aussie who lives most of the time in Texas and drove his '32 Ford Tudor to Bonneville for Speed Week 2021.

ABOVE: Another shot of the street rodders enjoying their time at the salt. From the length of the shadows you can tell that this photo was obviously taken early in the morning, a great time to be on the salt, before it gets too hot. Later in the day most of the visitors adjourn to the car park at the Golden Nugget Casino.

BONNEVILLE
SPEED WEEK 2021

started on the Saturday and Speed Week soon settled into its rhythm with over 200 passes on the first day, and 29 qualifiers waiting in impound at the end of the day. Salt conditions were near perfect after a dry winter and spring in the area. Unfortunately there were some serious accidents at Speed Week this year with drivers injured.

However, the near perfect racing conditions resulted in over 100 new records being set by the end of the week, one of the best results for Speed Week for some time. Once again Speed Demon set the fastest speed of the meet, going 466.290 mph on the Sunday running in A/BFS class, but damaging the engine in the process and not being able to back it up for that class. They fitted a smaller engine and went racing again in E/BFS and still went 390.952 mph!

The J&S Racing team were also competing in A/BFS class and put down a strong run at 410.635 mph – any vehicle that can top 400 mph on Bonneville is really moving. To watch such runs in person is to experience a sound and experience like no other. It feels like the earth is rotating beneath your feet when a streamliner passes the pits at this kind of speed.

Another team to do well was the Ferguson Racing streamliner with Danny Thompson driving. They recorded a fastest speed of 388.740 mph. At the end of this coverage is a list of the new record holders (four wheel vehicles only – for motorcycle records and all other results see the website <scta-bni.org>).

LEFT: Just the thing for some fun on the salt at Bonneville, a fenderless, banger powered Model A tourer with non-standard grille shell, lengthened hood and wonky headlight.

BELOW: If you like old Model A roadsters with patina then this black one might light your fire. It sports wire wheels and headlights off a '35 Ford with a dropped headlight bar about the only other concession to hot rodding.

LEFT: Jack Rogers' Camaro has been to Lake Gairdner on a couple of occasions as well as being a regular competitor at Bonneville where he ran 247.296 mph this year.
BELOW: The Gearhead Guru Racing C/STR '34 roadster is a fast car at 214.177 mph.

www.graffitipub.com.au

ABOVE: Why not use your rare '31 Model A roadster pickup as a tender vehicle at the salt? The pickup bed is ideal for all those things you need at the start line.

ABOVE: Looks like this '32 Ford Tudor is still a work in progress.

ABOVE: Once again the Speed Demon was fastest of the long, sleek streamliners with a 466.290 mph pass in A/BFS class that unfortunately damaged their big engine, so in went the smaller version and they still went 390.952 mph later in the week in E/BFS class.

RIGHT: Hard, dry salt conditions meant it wasn't such a drama to take your good street rod out on the lake this year. When it is a little damp lots of salt gets thrown all over (and under) the car.

BELOW: J & S Racing was the second fastest team at Bonneville this year, posting a best speed of 410.635 mph in their long grey streamliner, also running in A/BFS class.

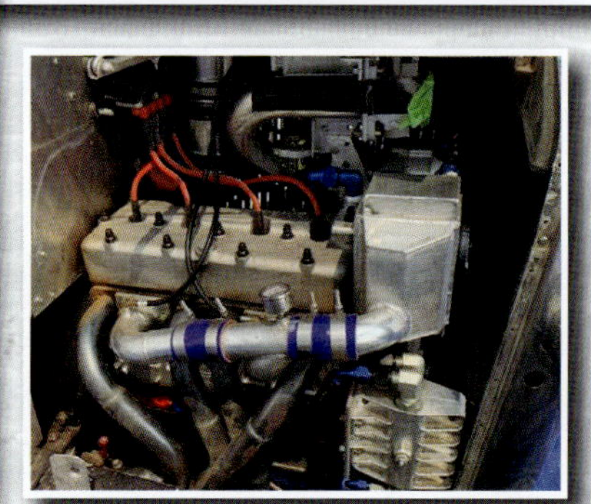

ABOVE & LEFT: The 4 Ever 4 club members take their Bonneville racing seriously and get serious results. The bellytank had a wildly modified banger engine this year and laid down a strong 174 mph run before the engine went away. Larry Madole also ran the Model coupe that knocked out a speed of 87.989 mph in V4F/BVGC class, not too shabby for a banger engine pushing a square, wind resisting fully fendered coupe body.

ABOVE: Bowman & Beck are regulars at Bonneville in their #811 Model A Ford roadster that went 193.072 mph this year.

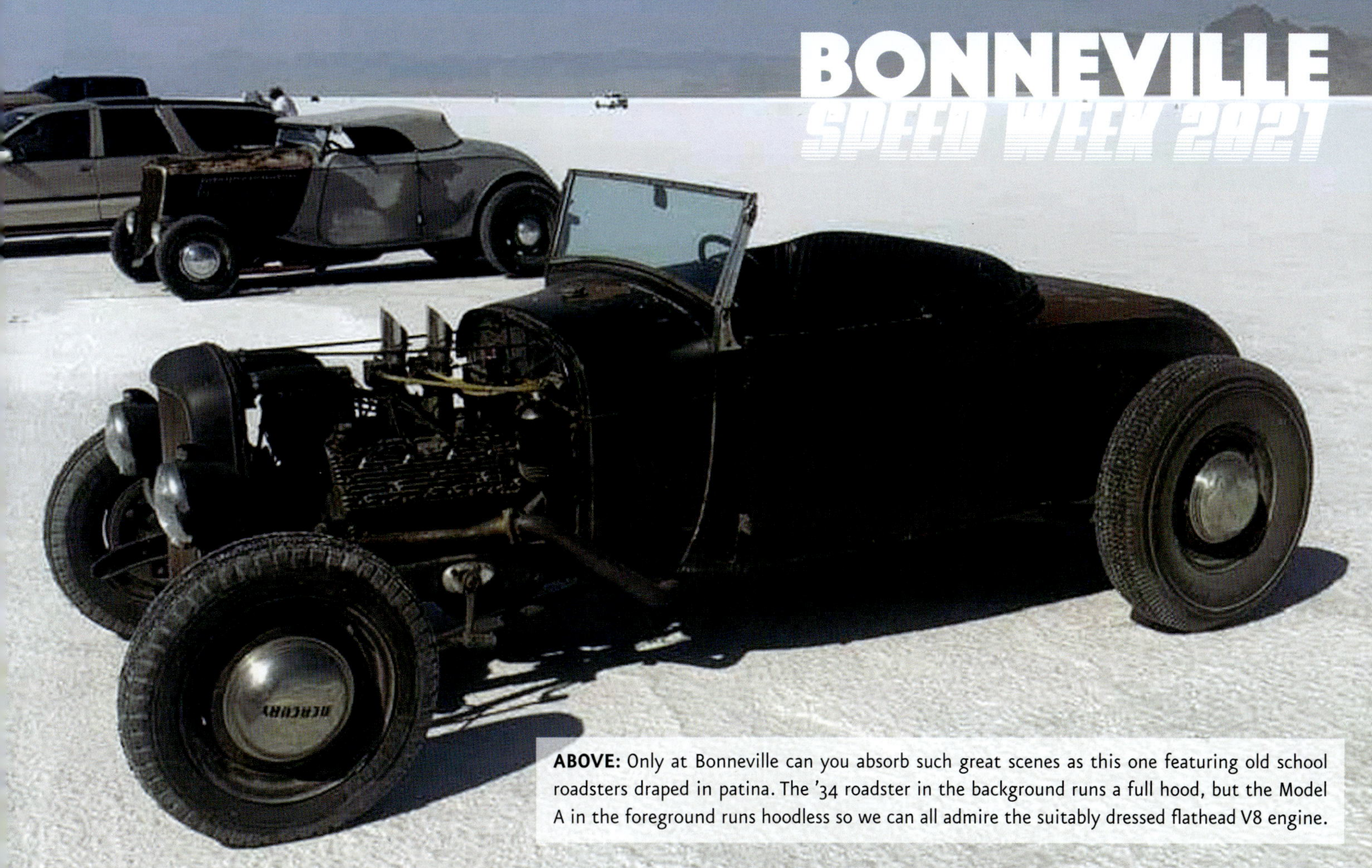

ABOVE: Only at Bonneville can you absorb such great scenes as this one featuring old school roadsters draped in patina. The '34 roadster in the background runs a full hood, but the Model A in the foreground runs hoodless so we can all admire the suitably dressed flathead V8 engine.

BONNEVILLE CERTIFIED NEW RECORDS - SPEED WEEK (SPEEDS IN MPH)

NO	ENTRY NAME	CLASS	RECORD	DRIVER NAME	NO	ENTRY NAME	CLASS	RECORD	DRIVER NAME
44	DRM Racing	C FL	292.201	P. Prentice	916	Deans Thundersalt	2 AA BGRMR	262.685	B. Dean
66	BMR Racing	B FR	307.401	E. Marlen	987	WGB Valley Fever Real Street Racing	F BGS	316.299	J. Meagher
75	Ferguson Racing	B FS	350.589	D. Thompson	1000	Bockscar	I BGL	221.956	J. Steele
75	Ferguson Racing	B FS	385.561	D. Thompson	1000	Bockscar	I BGL	224.223	J. Steele
84	So What Speed Shop	A BGRMR	166.525	S. Hanchard	1205	That Guy Racing	K BGL	138.226	B. Daily
84	So What Speed Shop	A BGRMR	169.917	S. Hanchard	1429	Hot Rod Hoodlums	C BGRMR	263.286	L. Dickerson
123	Erik Hansson	XF BFR	195.286	R. Lundring	1636	BC Landspeed Racing	AA CBFALT	273.117	R. Beckman
132	Hansson & Palagyi	XXF BFL	244.188	R. Palagyi	1660	Montana Dodge Boys Lakester	XXF BGL	209.721	C. King
192	Wagon a Go-Go	G CGALT	133.798	D. Mellott	1761	RGS Motorsports	F FR	204.074	R. Sirna
218	Eight In A Row Racing	XO BFR	175.641	R. Foehner	1815	Ron's Hobby Shop Special	XF BFRMR	206.249	J. Arnett
313	Steve Lautug	V4F GL	152.850	S. Lautug	1921	Wagon A Gogo	G CGC	131.349	S. Harrison
363	Rydin Decal Racing	AA BGALT	256.298	J. Bell	1951	Marino-Batto	XO BFR	162.218	R. Marino
388	MRJ Racing	XO GMP	141.174	M. Miller	1997	SS & PF Racing	D MGT	223.579	T. Dean
418	Pilgrim & Stubbs	C DT	220.226	D. Pilgrim	2000	Logan's Run	A FMP	165.895	L. Maring
426	Flying Rose Racing	D BGRMR	177.776	J. Wollenberg	2571	Potter Brothers	G BGC	214.552	D. Potter
426	Flying Rose Racing	D BGRMR	198.503	J. Wollenberg	2588	Jesel Landspeed Team	E BFMP	241.463	S. Watt
497	David Hlebichuk	C MGT	226.854	C. Henderson	3522	I.C.E. Racing	G GC	193.550	J. Iliff
506	Wolfe - Strasburg	C BFL	361.201	A. Strasburg	4449	Jesel Landspeed Team	D BFMP	232.700	J. Barton
545	Screamin' Mimi Racing	XF GMR	166.354	P.Tolley	4449	Jesel Landspeed Team	D BFMP	253.438	J. Barton
623	Haines & Harte Saline Solution	XO BGL 2	243.784	J. Harte	4555	Shazam Racing	I GT	125.146	G. Gray
651	Gary Matranga	AA BGCC	291.215	G. Matranga	4555	Shazam Racing	I GT	127.225	G. Gray
660	Montana Dodge Boys Lakester	XXF BFL	230.829	P. Hendrickson	5005	Empire Special	B BGMR	289.199	J. Wirth
672	Salty Frog Racing	G DT	165.458	D. Hake	5037	Hagee Motorsports	C BGMMP	207.481	J. Minneker
672	Salty Frog Racing	G DT	171.992	D. Hake	5037	Hagee Motorsports	C BGMMP	198.401	J. Minneker
688	Lil Bit O Racing	E FMP	151.024	L. Lancaster	5048	Hagee Motorsports	C BGMMP	207.349	M. Defever
711	Chet Thomas Racing	B BSTR	251.735	D. Conley	5811	Oritz Family Racing	G CBGALT	169.426	M. Ortiz
723	Kowalski Special	V4F FRMR	97.858	E. Kowalski	7230	Kowalski Racing	V4F GRMR	105.479	EJ Kowalski
727	Anderson Prothero	B PRO	233.268	J. Anderson	7231	Kowalski Venza Santiago	V4 GRMR	98.291	M. Santiago
743	McFaddin & Loyd Racing	E CBGALT	219.788	A. Loyd	7232	Kowalski Racing	V4F VOT	112.427	EJ. Kowalski
751	Stewart Family Mustang	C FALT	244.929	G. Stewart	7761	Perley Motorsports	C GMMP	237.946	J. Perley
761	RGS Motorsports	F GR	198.812	R. Sirna	8150	Ron's Hobby Shop Special	XF BGRMR	205.744	R. San Giovanni SR
853	Black Creek Racing	XF BFMP	117.892	R.Thomas	8522	I.C.E. Racing	G FALT	191.834	J. Iliff
853	Black Creek Racing	XF BFMP	121.464	R.Thomas	9996	Salt Cat Racing	XO BFALT	181.136	D. Grieve

The Memory

Drag Racing in the sixties comes alive in living colour from the Mayo Collection

RIGHT: Classic photo of Ash Marshall and Valvoline promo girl sitting in the Vandal dragster gives a real feel for the Melbourne drag racing scene in 1965.

BELOW: Smoking the tyres is Colin Hyams in the ex Reg Hunt Maserati A6GCM racing car that was owned by several different people in Australia but ended up back in Switzerland. Imagine what it's worth now!

Kevin Mayo was right on the spot when Australian drag racing was emerging as a legitimate motor sport, both as a competitor and an official with the Victorian Hot Rod Association, the body that ran the early drag racing meetings in Victoria. Fortunately Kevin often carried his camera to these events and recorded much of the activity in colour slides, when most people were still only using black and white film. Brought to life by the wonders of modern scanning, here in printed form is Kevin's Memory Collection for us all to enjoy.

RIGHT: John English puts a hole-shot on an FX Holden competitor in the B/GS class. This is very early in the days of Riverside as John's scrawled number is 7, later to become number 1 when he won the pointscore series. The roadster also uses steel wheels, later his own alloy wheels.

BELOW: Kevin Mayo's own dragster was this tidy flathead-powered rail-equipped with quad Stromberg 97 carbies and bodywork that enclosed the roll cage.

BELOW LEFT: The Eagles were the second club to be formed in Victoria after the Southern Hot Rod Club and they operated a free repair service for the racers at Riverside.

BELOW RIGHT: Graham "Happy" Rose with his pit crew stand straight for an official team photo with Graham's triple SU equipped, six cylinder Holden powered dragster.

BELOW: Typical pit scene at Riverside captures the atmosphere and activity of the period. Apart from two VW beetles in the background every vehicle is Australian, American or British – how things have changed today!

RIGHT: Y block Ford-powered dragster was over from Adelaide and owned by Don Bradshaw. It used typical swept back zoomie headers and a sextet of Stromberg carbies.

MAIN PIC: Jack "Fizzball" Collins in Norm Beechey's six cylinder Holden powered rail gets the jump on Eddie Thomas' Chrysler powered dragster. Note the basic crowd control devices and the Melbourne city skyline in the background.

ABOVE: Dynospeed FJ Panel Van belonged to Max De Jersey, a regular competitor at early Riverside meets.

RIGHT: Dark blue, channelled '32 roadster uses flathead power with twin carbies and a neat nerf bar in front of a stock grille.

BELOW: The Mullins and Bell dragster from South Australia was built in the Chrysler workshops where Alf Mullins worked. It was sold to Barry Cordner in Melbourne and became known as the Mud Mouse. Look closely and you can see the block of wood used to make a blower manifold under the 6-71 blower.

BELOW: Darrol Finger's '34 Ford coupe was a regular competitor at Riverside. The car still exists and is owned by Ken Murphy who is currently rebuilding it.

MAIN PIC: Classic start line shot at Riverside with Tony Mullen's '32 Ford roadster up against the '34 Ford coupe of Hans Klemme.

ABOVE: Corvette special had twin four barrel equipped 327 small block Chevy engine in a space frame circuit racing chassis and belonged to Murray Carter. Driver protection was basic!

ABOVE: The first version of Peter Holder's dragster as mentioned at the top of the following page, without the towering induction setup. At this stage the flathead engine used a conventional tri-carb induction.

LEFT & BELOW: The "Flying Forest" was Peter Holder's spindly dragster that was easily recognised by its almost ridiculous home made ram tube induction with a quartet of Holley 94 carbs perched on top. This was the second version of Holder's dragster, the original version had a full width rear end and even spindlier roll cage. Note the friction shock absorbers used on the front end and clear view of the cockpit in the second view. Early dragsters were very basic, but no doubt lots of fun.

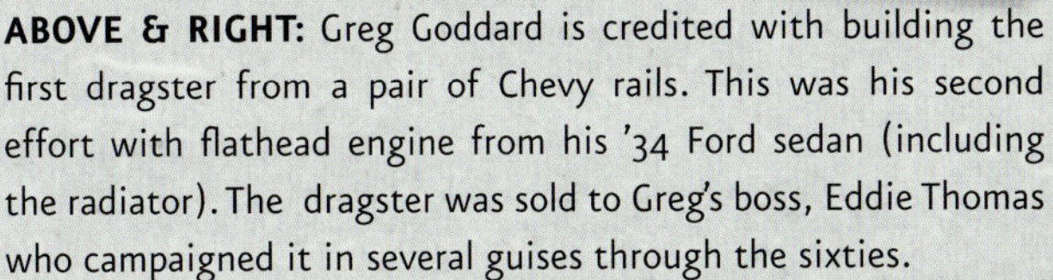

ABOVE & RIGHT: Greg Goddard is credited with building the first dragster from a pair of Chevy rails. This was his second effort with flathead engine from his '34 Ford sedan (including the radiator). The dragster was sold to Greg's boss, Eddie Thomas who campaigned it in several guises through the sixties.

ABOVE: Side view of Tony Mullen smoking away from the start line at Riverside in his popular and quick '32 Ford roadster that ran quad carb equipped Y block Ford engine and typical chromed steel wheels of the period.
BELOW: Imported Plymouth Ramchargers were the big performers in the tin-top ranks. The red one was raced at Riverside by Geoff Laver, while the darker example was raced by Max Stephens.

BELOW: Several photos of the Eddie Thomas dragster on its first outing with Chrysler wedge engine. At this stage it was still driven by John English, seen crouching in the lower photo, but inadequate braking for the new, more powerful overhead valve engine resulted in the dragster running off the end of the strip into ankle deep water. That was enough for English who refused to drive the dragster any more, so Thomas took over the drivng chores and stayed there for many years.

MAIN PIC: Obviously taken at the same time as our intro photo for this feature, this photo shows Ash Marshall with the Valvoline promo girl sittng in the Vandal dragster, but there is lots of interesting action in the background. Gathering up his parachute to the right is Graham Withers, the crewman on the right is Pat Ratcliff of the Eddie Thomas team which is approaching in the background with Eddie sitting in his dragster (Mk2), being pushed by an FX Holden ute. Once again we have a typical sixties Melbourne crowd and in the far background the vastly different skyline of the city compared to how it looks today.

BELOW: The Goddard (later Thomas) dragster scoots through the timers at the end of the strip at considerable speed with only a few hay bales and good luck separating it from the timing crew at the finish. Safety requirements were basic at best in these early days of drag racing at Riverside.

ABOVE: It was a big deal to have the first overhead valve engine in a dragster, so Len Case and Ray Spragge teamed up to drop the Chrysler engine out of Spragge's street roadster into Len's dragster in an overnight thrash. They succeeded, but their signwriter must have been suffering a hangover – the sign on the tank was meant to read "Sloppy Tune"

LEFT: Darryl Harvey's '34 Ford roadster at speed with Y block Ford power. The car still exists, basically as shown here.

BELOW: JohnMaher pushes up to the start line at Castlereagh in his injected hemi powered rail, courtesy of a near new two tone HD Holden sedan. In the background is the "Quarterhorse" Fiat alteredbeing pushed out of the pits to the start line.

BELOW: Little B/Gas Fiat Topolino sitting in the pits at Castlereagh. It appears to be Y Block Ford powered, as were many Aussie race cars then.

LEFT: Following the slingshot dragsters for popularity in early Australian drag racing were the altereds, like Chuck May's "Outcast". This one used a sextet of carbies on a big block Ford engine with typical zoomie headers and high riding stance in an effort to gain weight transfer off the line.

RIGHT: Yellow Fang was Ed Roth's radical dragster with finned bodywork and blown hemi engine. Roth never came out with the dragster, so it was driven by George Schrieber (pointing) while in Australia. Young Aussie drag fans were mesmerised by the Yellow Fang and this one event probably changed many of their lives forever.

ABOVE: Hot rods and street cars await their turn to race down the Castlereagh strip. The black Model A roadster was owned by Mike O'Sullivan a regular competitor at Castlereagh.

ABOVE: American visitor, Tony Nancy wowed the crowds at Castlereagh with his radical rear engine dragster that was really ahead of its time. It was blown Oldsmobile powered.

LEFT & ABOVE: More shots of Roth's Yellow Fang in the pits at Castlereagh and preparing for a run down the strip during Dragfest. Note the crowds in the backgrounds of nearly all of these photos, Aussies turned out in force to see the American dragsters run.

ABOVE: Another one of the American racers that came for Dragfest was Bob Mayer with his "Nightmayer" dragster. The blown hemi powered rail was a strong performer during the series at Castlereagh and Surfers Paradise strips.

ABOVE & MAIN PIC: George Stewart altered the wheelbase of his VW racer slightly and turned it into a high performance wheelstander that really brought the crowd to life. George was a regular competitor at Riverside and Calder Park strips, but these photos were taken at Castlereagh.

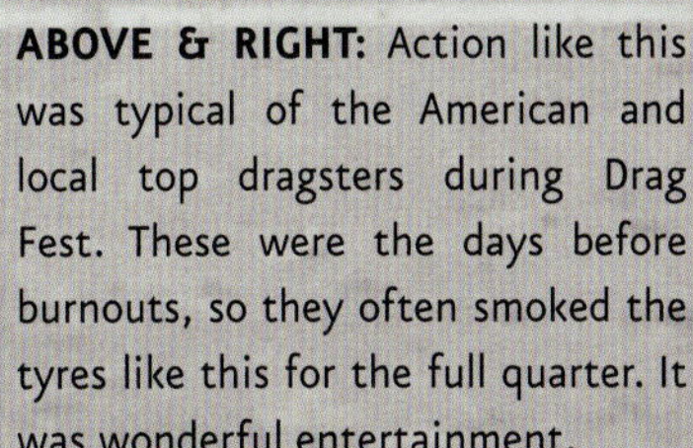

ABOVE & RIGHT: Action like this was typical of the American and local top dragsters during Drag Fest. These were the days before burnouts, so they often smoked the tyres like this for the full quarter. It was wonderful entertainment.

LEFT: King of the hot rods in Sydney was Dennis Walford's magenta metalflake T bucket that sported black interior trim and healthy Y block Ford power with individaul trumpet shaped zoomie headers.

MAIN PIC: Locals Aussie racers Ash Marshall and Graham Withers had many closely matched races in their top dragsters. Ash's "Vandal" in the left lane and Graham's still red version in the right lane. Ampol sponsorship saw the Withers rail painted white soon after.

BOTTOM: Weird looking Model A Ford coupe based altered was raced by Roger Keogh using Y block Ford running gear.

BELOW: Typical flathead engine of sixties Aussie drag racing has now highly collectible, locally made Waggott heads and four Holley 94 two barrel carbies on a Weiand intake manifold. Love the copper venturi toppers on the carbies! Imagine this in a roadster now.

LEFT: "Torque-e" Fiat Topolino B/Gasser has what appears to be a twin cam Jaguar six engine buried deep in the firewall for better weight distribution.

BELOW: Warren Armour was a regular racer at Castlereagh where he had several cars including this six cylinder dragster with Fiat Topolini body dropped over the top to put it into the experimental and short-lived Competition Dragster class.

BELOW: This scene from the Castlereagh pits is typical of almost any early Australian drag strip where the majority of the sling-shot rails were six cylinder Holden powered.

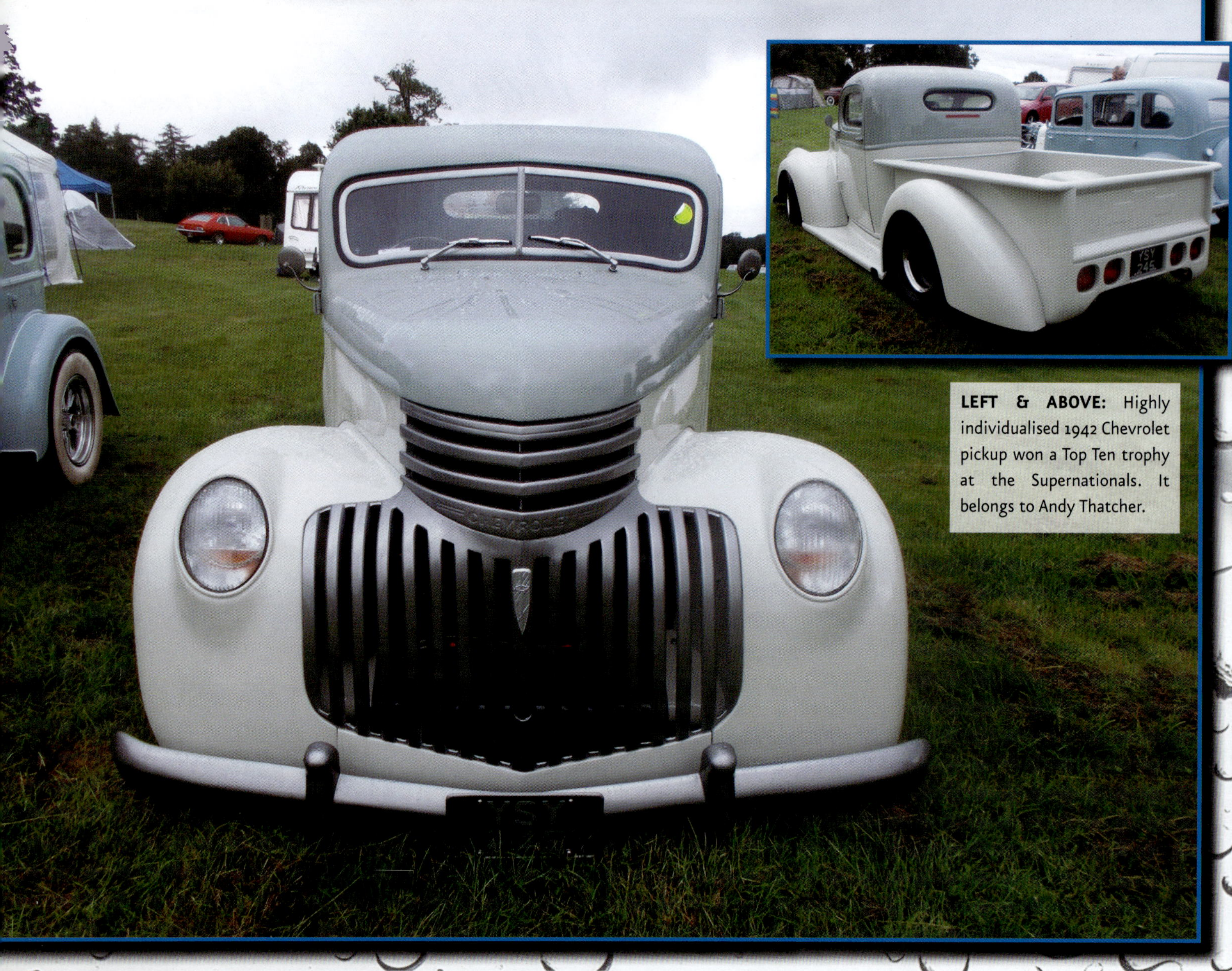

The NSRA Hot Rod Supernationals is one of the highlights of the UK rodding scene and after being closed down during the worst of the COVID-19 pandemic it was back for 2021 on the weekend of 5-8 August at its normal home of Old Warden in Bedfordshire. It's no surprise the format had to be down-sized compared to past Supernationals, particularly with regard to spectators, but it still featured enough of the right ingredients to give participants a fantastic weekend. The cars were still the stars of the show, the participants were eager to share some time together, and there was a great atmosphere. That all adds up to another super Supernationals.

The lead up to the event posed many logistical challenges for the NSRA's event organising team. A new entrance road into the venue meant a rethink of the way the registration system could be organised. There were COVID-19 precautions to implement, including having all camping units individually marked and sited for health and safety reasons. That was a mammoth task as there were over 800 tent sites required! However, the hard working NSRA committee, crew, and helpers, coped with it all and as a result, the event was another great success.

COVID regulations required that this was a NSRA members-only event, with exception of limited numbers of members' guests. The event had to be pre-entry only, numbers were limited, the NSRA were not able to take payment on the gate and no cash sales were available.

Individual NSRA members were allowed one guest, whereas family members could have two guests – however both family members had to be present for both guests to be allowed in.

Tickets were £60 per person for the weekend and only for the full Thursday to Sunday period.

Participants could still attend the Sunday show and shine only, but again, this was only available by pre-entry, and had to be a no-cash-at-the-gate situation for the NSRA. There were limited facilities, for things like entertainment, toilets, showers etc.

Entrants were still able to order event T-shirts as part of their booking and they were available for collection in the hospitality tent at the event.

Camping areas were allocated on arrival, but there was still the opportunity to book an area you wished to camp in, such as Disabled, Quiet or General camping, Hill camping and camping for vehicles over 10 metres in length.

Overall it was another great success for the NSRA Supernationals and plans are already in motion for the 2022 Hot Rod Supernationals as it coincides with the 50th anniversary of the NSRA!

ABOVE RIGHT: Yellow '32 Ford five window coupe looks just right with flipper caps on painted steel wheels and Moon tank out front.

RIGHT: You can tell from this photo of a red '62 Chevy sedan that the weather wasn't very kind in the early part of the event.

BELOW: Alan Marsh won the "Shuttleworth Pick" trophy for his '37 Dodge pickup. Alan has been a regular supporter of the Supernats for many years.

Words: Larry O'Toole
Photos: Nick Darling

LEFT: We don't often see this model Dodge pickup as a ground hugging street custom. It's a '55 C-3B model with wrap-around windshield and big back window option.

BELOW: Bright red Dodge Dart has large hood scoop and rear wheel cut-outs to give the vehicle a street-strip image.

ABOVE: For sale at a reduced price of £16,000.00, this chopped and channelled custom pickup, "Taxirod" with blown 350 Chevy power uses a 8.8 Ford rear axle and was built from a London Taxi!

BELOW: Custom C cab T model with blown Daimler Hemi running gear and a Jag rear end is a uniquely English street rod. If those megaphone header collectors are straight through, you will definitely hear it coming!

RIGHT: Clean looking 1941 Ford pickup looks great riding on chrome wheels with hubcaps and is left hand drive, indicating it might have been imported from the USA.

BELOW: Pop two door sedan looks tidy in soft grey finish with Center Line wheels and dark tinted windows. Naturally, the home-grown Ford Populars are just that in the UK and even have their own display area at the Supernats.

BELOW RIGHT: Jake and Niamh's 1957 Austin A55 Cambridge Mk I is a tongue-in-cheek "custom" with 1.6 B Series engine and four speed transmission – just for fun!

ABOVE: Vauxhall sedan in two tone blue with whitewalls on polished alloy wheels looks every bit a cool custom.

BELOW: Dodge Polara station wagon has more than enough space to take along everything you need for a weekend at the Supernats.

ABOVE: Looking like it is fresh from the farm is this '63 Chevy Styleside pickup, ready for work or play.

BELOW: GMC Pickup is a 1956 model that has been completely dechromed and bathed in medium grey.

ABOVE: Plymouth Valiant two door sedan would be a rare car in the UK and quite different to the Australian made versions of the same model Valiant.

LEFT: Heavily channelled Model A Ford four door sedan sits super low with radical top chop, Mopar V8 engine and early Ford wire wheels with whitewalls.

ABOVE: Ford Falcon Sprint rolls on American five spoke wheels and has tan interior trim.

RIGHT: This 1937 Rover 10 belongs to David Newman and features a Daimler 4.6 litre Hemi V8 topped with four carbies, a ZF four speed auto, Vauxhall Magnum rear end and Volvo 240 Dena front end.

BELOW: Green Ford Popular has air-dam style front sheet metal treatment and monster hood scoop to give it a nasty competition look.

BELOW LEFT: Keith Smith took home the "Special award" chosen by John Price and of course, being John's pick, it was a Jag, a pro street style MK 10 to be precise.

BELOW: Bright red '30 Model A Tudor has chopped top, stout blown small block Ford engine and polished American five spoke wheels.

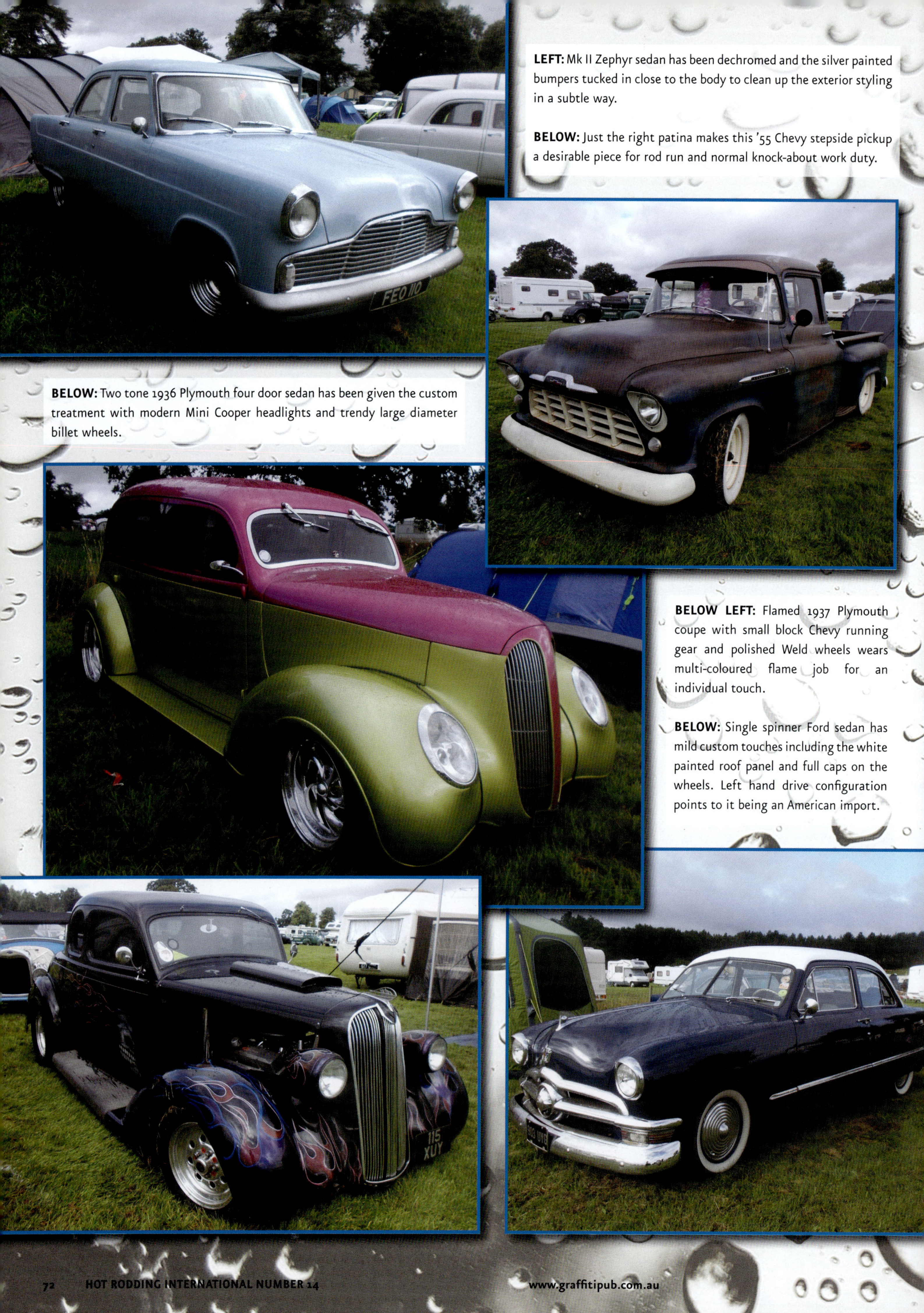

LEFT: Mk II Zephyr sedan has been dechromed and the silver painted bumpers tucked in close to the body to clean up the exterior styling in a subtle way.

BELOW: Just the right patina makes this '55 Chevy stepside pickup a desirable piece for rod run and normal knock-about work duty.

BELOW: Two tone 1936 Plymouth four door sedan has been given the custom treatment with modern Mini Cooper headlights and trendy large diameter billet wheels.

BELOW LEFT: Flamed 1937 Plymouth coupe with small block Chevy running gear and polished Weld wheels wears multi-coloured flame job for an individual touch.

BELOW: Single spinner Ford sedan has mild custom touches including the white painted roof panel and full caps on the wheels. Left hand drive configuration points to it being an American import.

ABOVE: Purple and bumperless 1940 Ford coupe sits in the soaking rain while the owners stay under in their tent.

RIGHT: Model A Tudor is a 1930 model done in fenderless style with blown small block Chevy running gear and a Deuce grille up front.

BELOW: Accessorised GMC pickup sits low thanks to air-bag suspension and looks like it might have been "born in the USA".

BELOW: Notch-back Anglia two door is flying the flag for locally made products with a custom make-over.

After a COVID induced break in 2020, the show scene burst back into action with the Sydney Hot Rod & Custom Auto Expo over the weekend of May 28-29, 2021. Patrons were treated to a high class show across three indoor sites and two outdoor areas, all packed with a fantastic array of custom built cars. The extended break meant a big increase in new cars – to the extent that unveilings had to be limited to 11 vehicles.

Highlights from the unveil cars included two amazing Holden Monaros from the Taree-based, Downtown Kustoms, three new street rods from Deluxe Rod Shop and Peter Gruyters' jaw-dropping bare metal Deuce coupe.

The show featured several special sections, such as Nostalgia Lane and the drive in show and shine area for day visitors' vehicles. Both were filled to capacity and featured a wide array of hot rods and customs, especially Nostalgia Lane. This area of the show was full of period correct traditional hot rods, customs, lowriders and race cars along with a few vendors that cater specifically to these styles. Add in the trade and demonstration area under the betting ring roof and you have a complete package to suit everyone.

Tool and equipment demonstrations, pinstripers and air brush artists gave visitors a look into how aspects of custom car building are achieved while vendors catering to fashion, parts and accessories littered other areas of the show floors. There was a pinup style pageant held during the show and a Bike Build Off comp. Rounding out the program were engine start-ups by the AC Delco Monaro doorslammer and a V12 Merlin hydroplane.

Crowd numbers were very strong all weekend, enjoying the wonderful display of cars and trade stands. Come presentation time the big winners were Peter Sharp with his HQ Monaro taking out Top Car of the Show, Brian Imlach won Top Street Rod with his stunning '34 Chev, Dean Rickard with his HT Monaro won Top Street Machine and Peter Gruyters, who took home both the Austin Arrowsmith Elegance Award and the Kevin Daley Memorial Award with his 572 Ford Boss powered Deuce coupe. Other winners worthy of a mention were Jason Kennedy's flamed Single Spinner winning Top Custom, Max McGinnis' '39 Chev taking out Top Lowrider and the Northern Beaches Hot Rod Club, who won the award for Best Club Display with their neat beach-themed stand. ◼

Words: Larry O'Toole Photos: Al O'Toole

ABOVE: Steve McDonald brought his 1931 Ford coupe up from Victoria for the show. The blown 355 Chevy powered Model A features an XJ6 Jaguar rear end, Cragar wheels and a Deuce grille. It won the Street Rod awards for Top Undercarriage, Top Trim and First Place in the Coupe class.

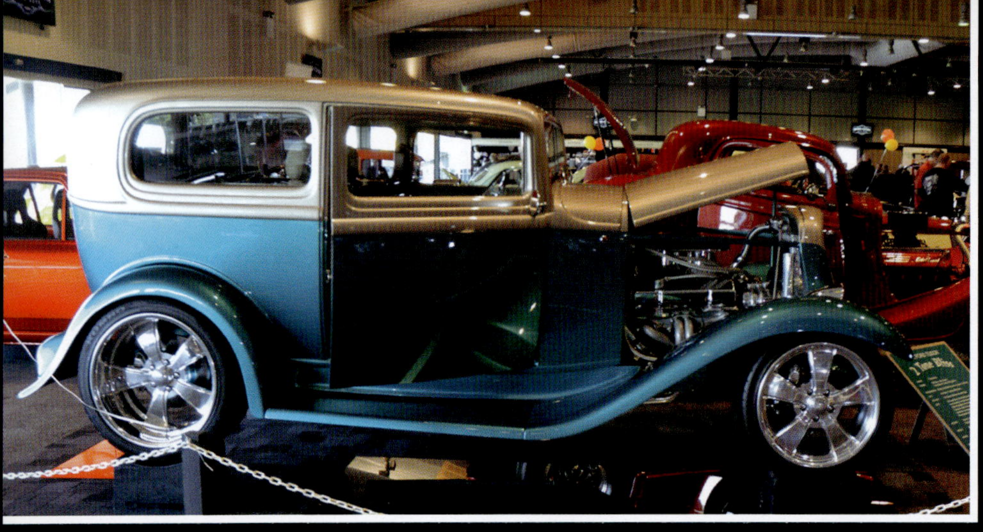

ABOVE: Chris Abela from the Idle Wild Hot Rod Club had his superb Deuce Tudor on show amongst the club's display. It runs a 350 Chevy and features many custom modifications.
BELOW: Tony Portelli's big block Ford powered 1932, "Orange Deuce" wears Dupont 2 pak paint and a set of Weld wheels. This car has been on the road for over 20 years.

ABOVE: Winner of Top Custom Paint in the Street Rod class was Elie Hannoun with this wild '23 Ford T bucket. Elie also claimed Third Bucket with the blown Chevy motivated hot rod.
BELOW: Steven Frustaci's 1978 Holden LX Torana was unveiled at the beginning of the show and was judged Third in the Street Machine Two-Door, 1949-1984 category.

ABOVE: Another entry from Deluxe Rod Shop was Cheryl and Ron Mills' '32 Ford five window coupe. This red Deuce runs a fully built 347 Windsor, five speed Tremec 'box and American Rebel wheels.

graffitipub.com.au

LEFT: Down from Queensland was Robert Downing with his "So-Evl" custom hot rod. It was built using a custom '23 T bucket chassis and an all-steel Fiat Topolino that has been chopped, stretched and widened. It runs a Turbo 350 behind a 340 Chevy and sports American Racing Salt Flat Special wheels, green and white vinyl upholstery and House of Kolor Frost White paint with Anti-Freeze Green highlights.

ABOVE: Dave Hart built this 1946 Ford convertible for Maurie Evans over a 20 year period. It runs an XJ6 Jag front end 500 cubic inch Cadillac V8 backed by a TH400 Pontiac transmission and narrowed nine inch diff. The car has been chopped two and half inches, channelled two inches and the body shaved and de-chromed.

RIGHT & ABOVE RIGHT: Check out the clear perspex roof insert in this 1934 Ford sedan from the Idle Wild Hot Rod Club. It runs a 351 Cleveland, C4 and nine inch rear end.

BELOW: There's a 620 horsepower, 502 cubic inch fuel injected Ram Jet engine under the bonnet of Dale O'Neill's 1957 Chevy pickup. It rolls on 18x8 inch and 18x10 inch American Racing wheels and features American oak in the bed and leather upholstery in the cab.

ABOVE: Orange '23 T bucket belongs to Idle Wild Hot Rod Club life member, Don Attard. It sports twin Holley 600s atop a blown 350 Chevy backed by a two speed Powerglide and nine inch diff with light grey leather upholstery.

ABOVE & INSET: This bare metal Deuce coupe belongs to Peter and Anna Gruyters and took out the Austin Arrowsmith Elegance Award and the Kevin Daley Memorial Award. It boasts a 572 cubic inch Ford Boss motor equipped with FiTech EFI backed by a Tremec TKO five speed 'box and a Winters quick-change rear end. The interior features pleated leather trim while the body sports 701 louvres!

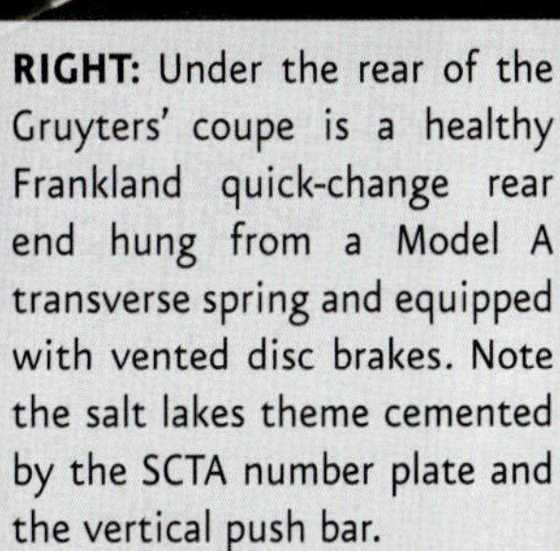

RIGHT: Under the rear of the Gruyters' coupe is a healthy Frankland quick-change rear end hung from a Model A transverse spring and equipped with vented disc brakes. Note the salt lakes theme cemented by the SCTA number plate and the vertical push bar.

ABOVE & MAIN: Tasmanian rodders, Brian and Maureen Imlach unveiled their superb '34 Chev sedan, built by the team at Deluxe Rod Shop. It won several awards including Top Street Rod and runs a blown LS2, Tremec six speed gearbox, nine inch rear and Billet Specialties wheels.

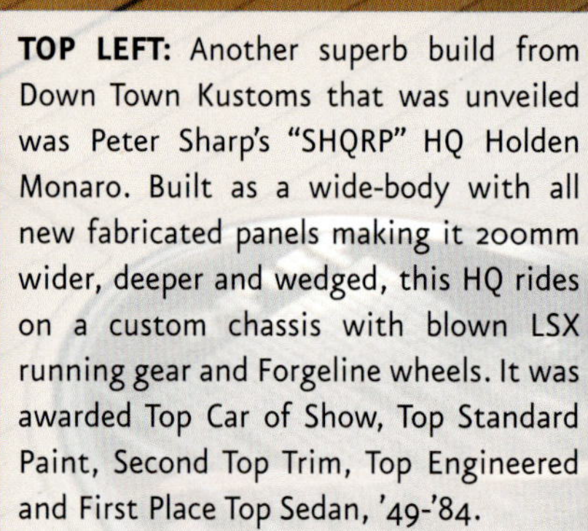

ABOVE: Down Town Kustoms brought along four cars for the show this year, two of which were brand new unveil cars. Dean Rickard's resto mod '69 HT Holden Monaro GTS runs a 6.2 litre LS3, a Tremec T56 Magnum six speed gearbox and a custom nine inch diff. It won Top Street Machine, along with Third Top Standard Paint, Third Top Undercarriage, Third Top Engine Bay, First Top Trim and Second Two Door, '49-'84.

TOP LEFT: Another superb build from Down Town Kustoms that was unveiled was Peter Sharp's "SHQRP" HQ Holden Monaro. Built as a wide-body with all new fabricated panels making it 200mm wider, deeper and wedged, this HQ rides on a custom chassis with blown LSX running gear and Forgeline wheels. It was awarded Top Car of Show, Top Standard Paint, Second Top Trim, Top Engineered and First Place Top Sedan, '49-'84.

ABOVE LEFT: Leonidas Mortakis' put this candy brown "Hardtop Demon" together using a 1969 VF Valiant and 440 big block running gear.

BELOW: The lush tan leather interior of the Imlach's Best Displayed Car-winning 1934 Chev sedan. It also won Second Top Trim in Street Rod class.

ABOVE: A beautifully detailed 8BA flathead with C4 Automatic transmission graces the engine bay of Mick Tyquin's '32 Charcoal Ford hiboy roadster.
BELOW: We don't see enough Chevy roadsters of the early '30s era like this 427 big block powered 1929 model with 31 spline nine inch rear end.

ABOVE: Gordon's one-inch chopped 1964 Buick Riviera, "Dorado" runs a stroked 425 Nailhead, T350 transmission and Mike Curtis wheels.
BELOW: Wild Willys coupe is actually street driven with Chevy 350/350 running gear despite its race car heritage and wild paint scheme.

BELOW & LEFT: Take an old Dodge ute and give it a retro rod make-over on a '35 Hudson chassis like Dodge Marshall (his real name!) did with his '39 model and you end up with an eye-catching hot rod. Beer barrels are the fuel tanks and the engine is a '64 Chrysler Poly 318 A.

ABOVE: Geoff Brown has done an outstanding job of combining the running gear and interior from a BA Falcon into his '56 F100 pickup truck.

BELOW: John Keighran's '56 Ford F100 with 260 Boss Ford motor and four speed auto has paint by the owner, trim by John Viles and Boyds wheels.

ABOVE: Flathead powered '33 Ford pickup looks great in silver and black.

BELOW: The Easy Street Rod & Custom Club's display theme was "The Delinquent Pickup Muster" that included Harry Smith's Mazda Red '40 Ford equipped with a 302 Windsor, C4 and nine inch diff with L300 front end.

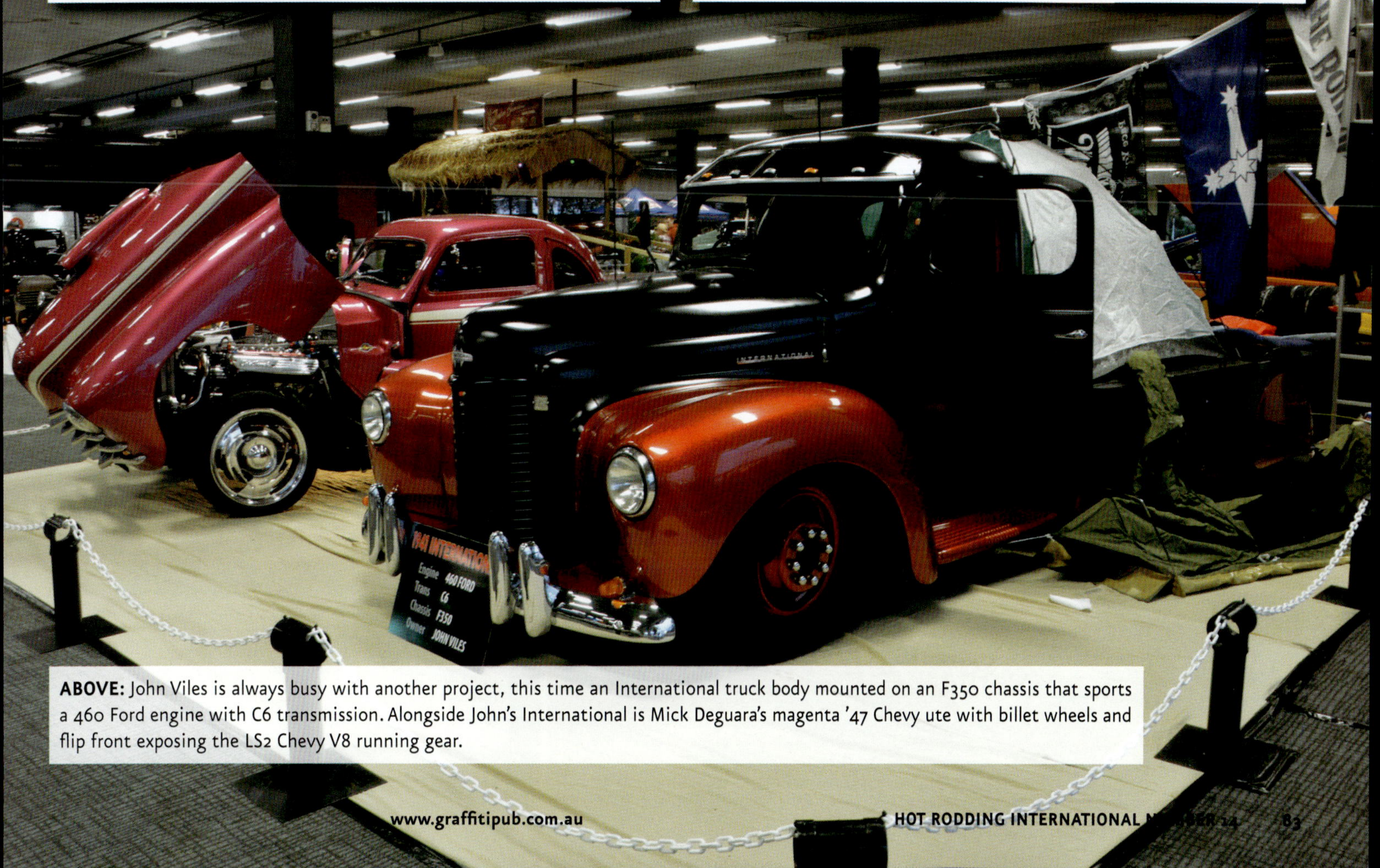

ABOVE: John Viles is always busy with another project, this time an International truck body mounted on an F350 chassis that sports a 460 Ford engine with C6 transmission. Alongside John's International is Mick Deguara's magenta '47 Chevy ute with billet wheels and flip front exposing the LS2 Chevy V8 running gear.

ABOVE: Unfinished but still outstanding with heaps of modifications, this '53 Chevy custom is being built by OG Customs for Matt Gatto.

LEFT: Peter and Jean Richards own their own version of the Munsters car, (based on a 1928 Chev tub) complete with coffin handles, severed arm holding the steering wheel and skeleton passenger in the back seat. Under all that induction is a 350 Chevy.

ABOVE: Black flames over yellow paint makes an eye-catching finish on the "NITRO34" Ford coupe.

ABOVE: Darko Gudelj has done an outstanding job of preserving the former Jim Suttar T bucket, right down to the Dave Hart murals and blown small block Chevy engine.

RIGHT: Jim Nicholson showed off his '23 T bucket that is based on a Total Performance kit from USA and runs a tunnel ram equipped small block Chevy engine with a dominant shotgun style scoop.

LEFT: Taipan Towing have the smartest tow truck in town, based on the chopped cabin of a '37 Ford pickup. It's 350 Chevy powered and features a custom made rear section and towing jib, runs large diameter billet wheels and has polished cycle fenders.

SYDNEY HR&C AUTO EXPO

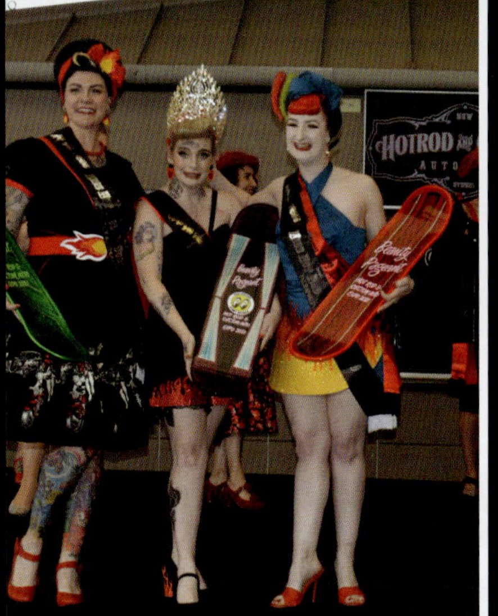

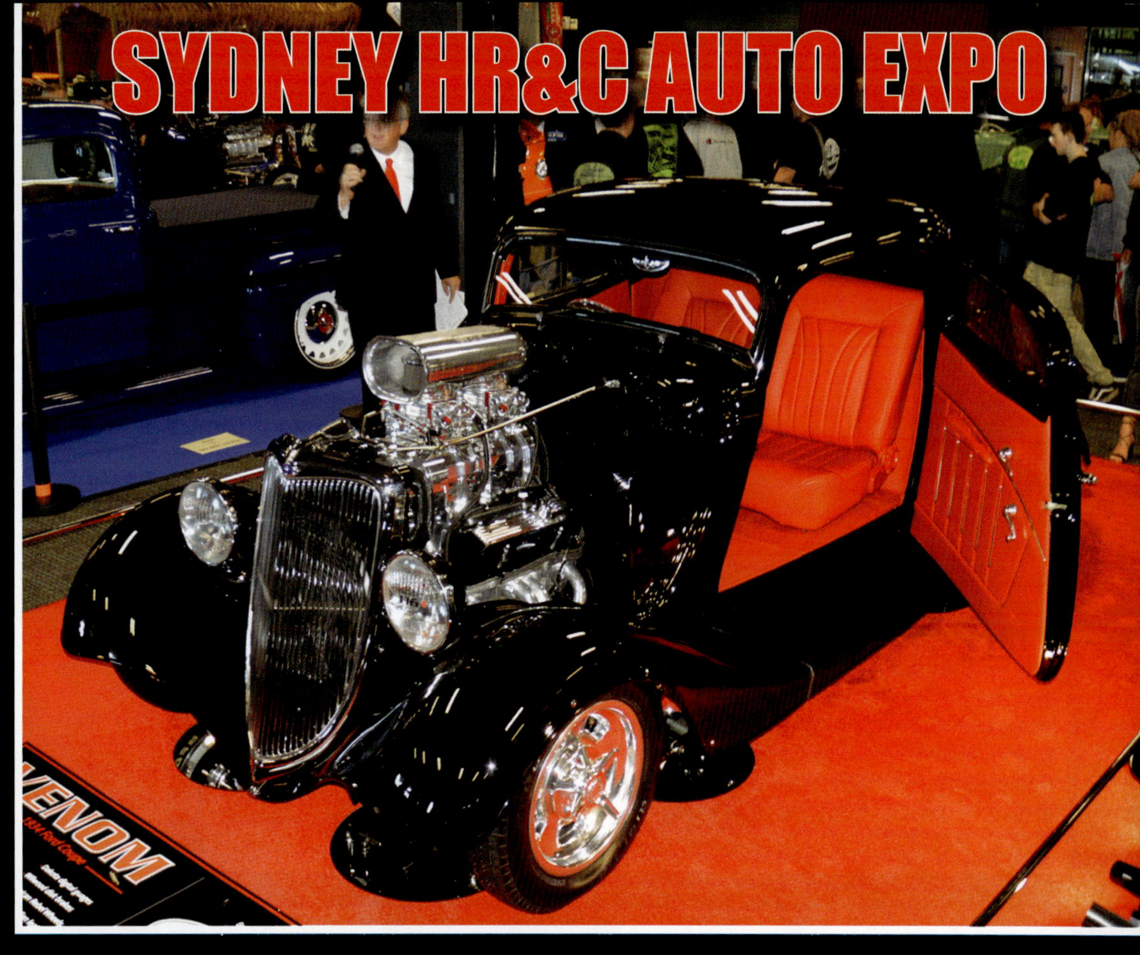

ABOVE: One of three unveil cars from Deluxe Rod Shop at the show, this tough '34 Ford coupe, "Venom" belongs to Matt Olver. It's been rebuilt in jet black paint using a blown 383 Chevy, Dakota Digital gauges, Wilwood disc brakes and American Rebel wheels. It won Third Top Engine Bay.

TOP LEFT: Scenes from the Hot Rod & Custom Auto Expo Pinup Pageant. Yes, it was vibrant!

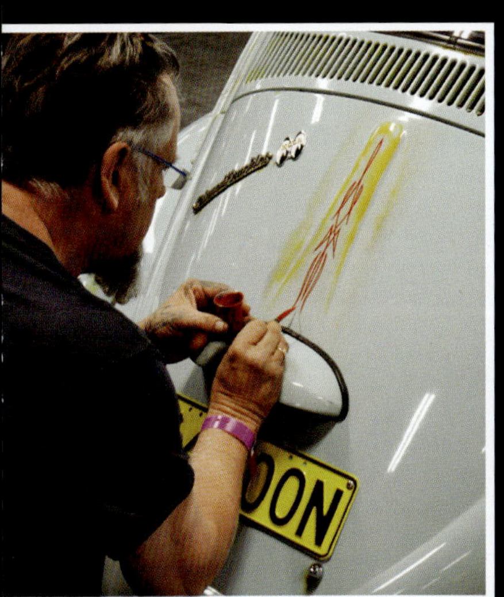

ABOVE: Tony "Airspeed" Marks laying down some lines on a VW hood.

BELOW: John McCoy-Lancaster interviews Greg Maskell about the neat '57 Chevy Nomad they have just witnessed being unveiled. The beautiful black and white Nomad is actually John's own vehicle.

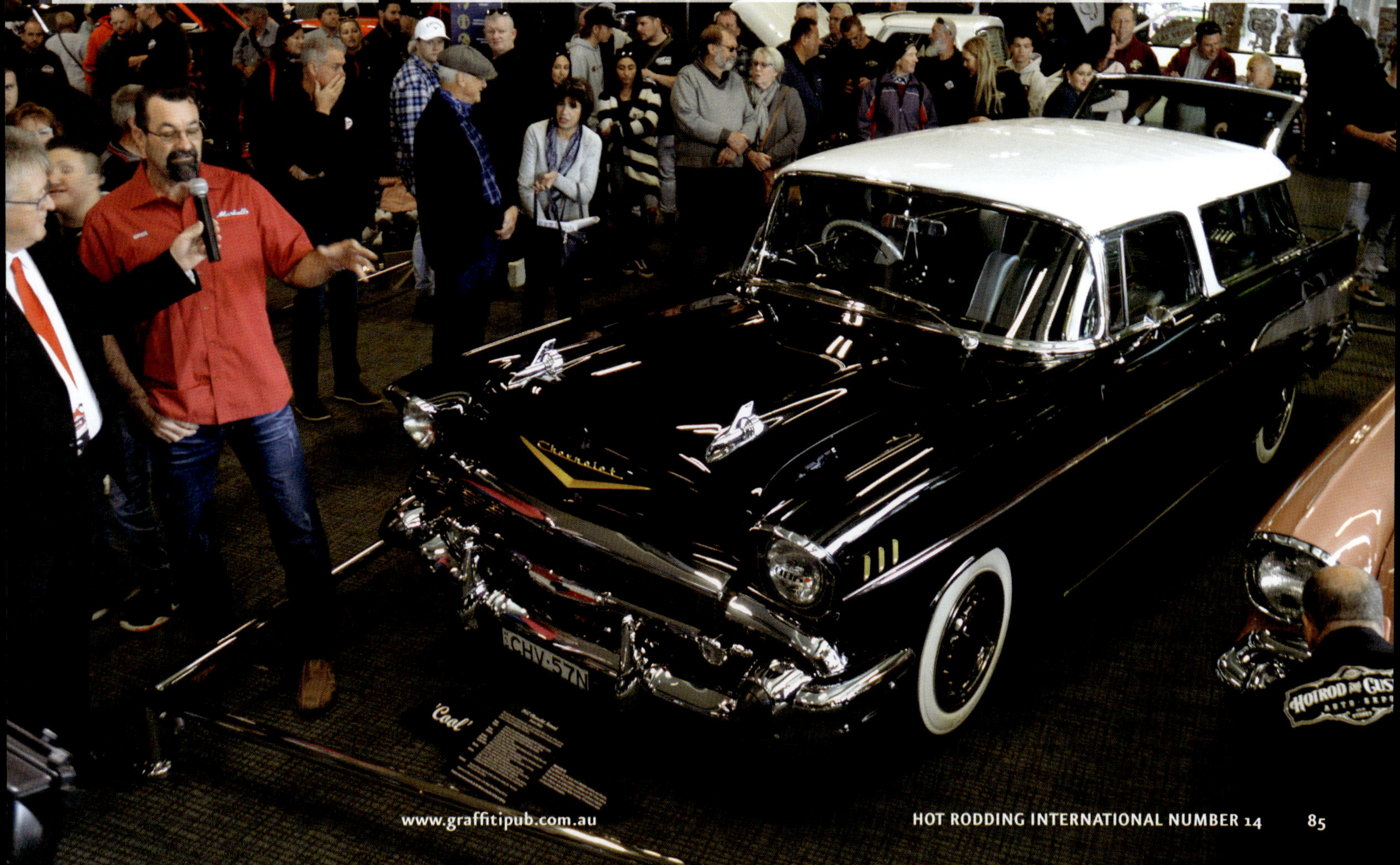

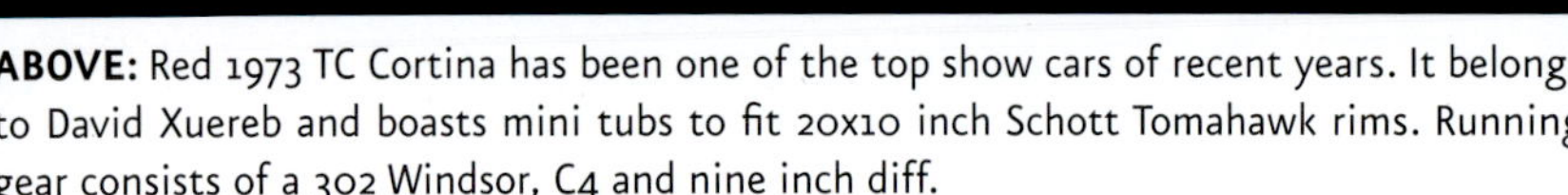

ABOVE: Red 1973 TC Cortina has been one of the top show cars of recent years. It belongs to David Xuereb and boasts mini tubs to fit 20x10 inch Schott Tomahawk rims. Running gear consists of a 302 Windsor, C4 and nine inch diff.

ABOVE RIGHT: First of the unveil cars was the Deuce hiboy roadster of Stephen Rich that features 383 small block Chevy engine and Winters quick-change rear end.

RIGHT: Up from Canberra was Alan Davies in his trusty '32 Ford three window coupe that is built hiboy style with Dodge Red Ram Hemi engine.

ABOVE: Two tone 1940 Ford roadster relies on a GM 6.2 litre LS3 engine and 6L80E transmission driving to a nine inch Tru Trac/LSD rear end.

ABOVE RIGHT: Tony and Janine Wilson's '32 Ford "CHOODA" has a Nankervis built, McGee injected 350 Chevy engine and is perfectly finished from end to end.

BELOW & RIGHT: Heading a line up of Romans rods is Steve and Lee Cordon's close to finished gold T coupe that sports many custom touches typical of '60s era show rods.

RIGHT: Dave and Sharon Dorman's Osborne bodied 1932 Ford Cabriolet looks superb in Lamborghini Giallo Maggio yellow paintwork with polished billet Foose Knuckle wheels shod with Kumho tyres. Inside is Italian black leather and Mercedes-Benz carpet. The Cabriolet also features independent front suspension and an S Type Jag rear end.

BELOW: If Kyle Smith's radically chopped and channelled '30 Model A Tudor looks vaguely familiar, perhaps it is because it has been given a makeover and now sports a black colour scheme with logos on the doors.

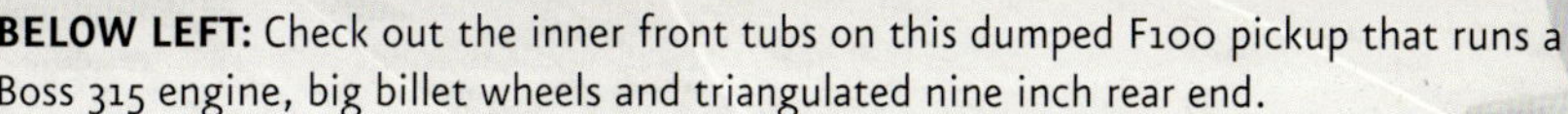

BELOW LEFT: Check out the inner front tubs on this dumped F100 pickup that runs a Boss 315 engine, big billet wheels and triangulated nine inch rear end.

BOTTOM LEFT: Dave and Lyn Keen own this amazing two door FJ Holden that was started by John Evers over 40 years ago. It has HQ Holden chassis under it and has been transformed by Down Town Kustoms, Hills and Co. and Trik Trim so you know it is a quality build.

BELOW: Andy's Ford Windsor powered '30 Model A Tudor is equipped with tunnel ram intake, four speed automatic transmission and Jag rear end.

ABOVE: We don't often see '64 Chevy station wagons in Australia so Gavin Knight's low-riding version certainly caught the eye of show patrons. Large diameter "Rallye" style wheels and low profile tyres work well on this one.

BELOW: Ardun headed sidevalve Ford engine in a Model A hiboy roadster with brown interior trim was typical of the displays in Nostalgia Lane.

LEFT: We spotted Romans Hot Rod Association club member, Kevin Kracht's '33 Ford Sports coupe, "El Tigre" in the visiting hot rodders parking area. It runs a 351 Windsor backed by a C4 auto and nine inch diff with caramel upholstery.

BELOW: Tony Thomas is onto a winning combination with his Model A roadster that runs a Hilborn injected four cylinder Mercruiser engine with five speed Supra transmission coupled to an open drive '48 Ford rear end equipped with a quick-change centre. The louvres on the deck lid and lower panel are repeated in a bellypan underneath.

ABOVE LEFT: "The Aggressor" was built in the sixties by David Tenny and runs a Rolls Royce Merlin V12 engine.

ABOVE: Keeping "The Aggressor" company is Brett and Wendy Howe's big block Chevy powered Everingham flat bottom boat "Atilla".

LEFT: Model A tourers aren't common as street rods these days but one with a 1950 Buick straight eight engine and built hiboy style is certainly different. Stuart Dunbar owns this beauty that sports a black fabric roof and painted steel wheels with polished hub caps.

BELOW: The daily drive in show area was populated with a fantastic collection of street driven rods and customs on both days of the show. This bright red XM Falcon hardtop was typical.

ABOVE: Blue '33 Ford hiboy roadster has a blown 351 Cleveland engine and highly polished Real Wheels. Inside is white leather and the roadster is fitted with a removable hard top for when the weather isn't so kind. Owner is Chris Krikorian from the Northern Beaches Hot Rod Club.

BELOW: Greeting show fans at the entry to Nostalgia Lane was the '33 Ford rcoupe of Dean Vanutinni, next to a bumperless 307 powered FE Holden that looks to be headed for the Nostalgia drag races and Ezio Cacciotti's Green Fing Plymouth Fury gasser.

ABOVE: Destruction is a chopped FB Holden wagon from the Road Devils Club that is a regular competitor at the Nostalgia Drags.

LEFT: Steve Alldrick built this delightful '32 Ford roadster for himself but his since sold it on to a new owner. Note the "factory" dressed 289 Ford Windsor and painted suspension components.

BELOW: Another Idle Wild club car on show was Richard Wehbe's Sunburst Orange 1934 Ford Tudor. It runs a 350/350 combo with a nine inch rear end.

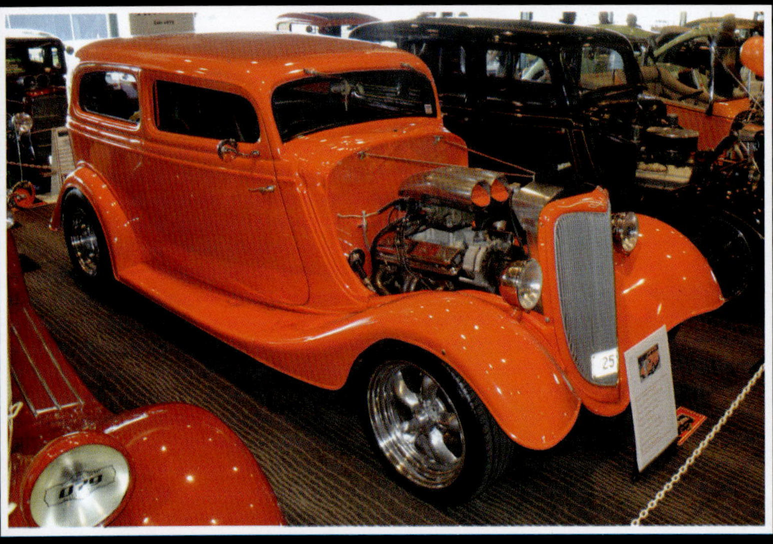

ABOVE: Damien Lewis travelled up from Victoria in his low-riding chopped, bare metal 1950 Ford custom that sports chrome wheels and whitewall tyres.

BELOW: Trevor Rockliff's orange T bucket looks perfect with nicely dressed 401 Buick Nailhead engine between the chassis rails with offset dual four barrel carbies and brown interior trim

BELOW: Basic and brown hiboy Deuce tourer looks racy with the windscreen folded back, rolls on black painted early Ford wire wheels and retains original style '32 Ford headlights.

ABOVE: Danny Dragosetti owns this outstanding purple Model A roadster that is stuffed full off blown 350 Chevy running gear.

ABOVE RIGHT: Take a '41 Willys coupe and stuff it full of blown Chevy engine and you have a winner every time. Greg Cooke from the Drag-Ens rod club owns this beauty.

BELOW: Another orange T bucket but this one is from Macquarie Towns Rod Club and it sports a small block Chevy engine.

ABOVE: Idle Wild Hot Rod Club member, Charles Vassallo is the proud owner of this slick 1930 Model A Ford coupe. It features blown 350 Chevy running gear and rolls on billet Dragway wheels.

ABOVE: Any XP Falcon sedan delivery will always attract attention, but put two of them side by side and you have a winning combination with the show patrons. Bevan Bolt owns the one on the right, no name on the other.

ABOVE: Chevy pickup with lazy axle rear end looks like a well-built work truck that must turn heads every time it is driven.
LEFT: Clayton Newham drove his late father, Col's five window Deuce to show alongside Harley Maric's Chevy powered '34 Ford coupe.

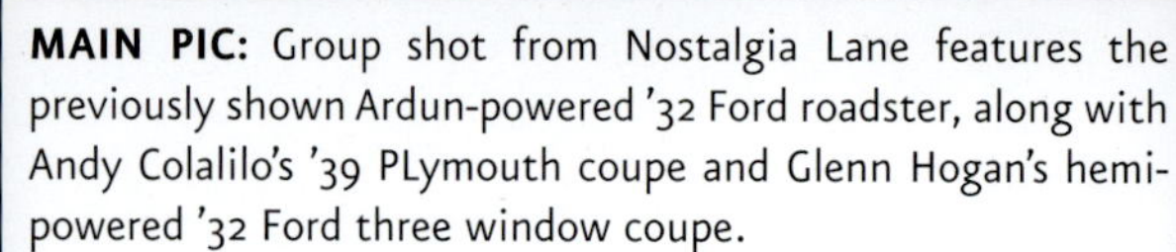

MAIN PIC: Group shot from Nostalgia Lane features the previously shown Ardun-powered '32 Ford roadster, along with Andy Colalilo's '39 PLymouth coupe and Glenn Hogan's hemi-powered '32 Ford three window coupe.

ABOVE: Unfinished but still outstanding with heaps of modifications, this '53 Chevy custom is being built by OG Customs for Matt Gatto

LEFT: Jason Kennedy owns the wildly flamed single spinner Ford that took home the Rod Lords Club Pick at trophy presentation time on Sunday afternoon.

BELOW: Matt Egan's chopped and panel painted Customline is an outstanding custom vehicle.

ABOVE: Norm Longfield's Model A Ford based woody speedster was parked among the outdoor daily show entarnts. Always one to turn out something different, Norm is still at it after decades of involvement in the hobby.

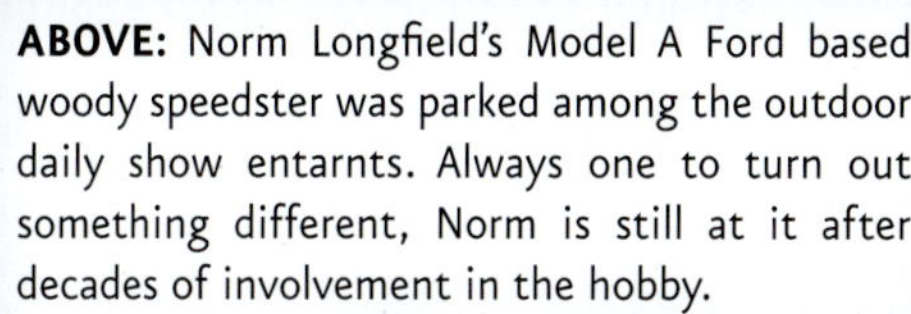

ABOVE: Promoter's Pick and Lucky's Pick awards went to Curtis Grima for his superbly turned out '62 Ford F100 pickup. It sits low, thanks to air-bag suspension and features outstanding custom panel painting all over the vehicle.

BELOW: The Marshall Speed Shop's nose up Willys gasser style coupe features hand built bodywork by Simon Allen and plenty of "Ruff 'n' Ready" attitude.

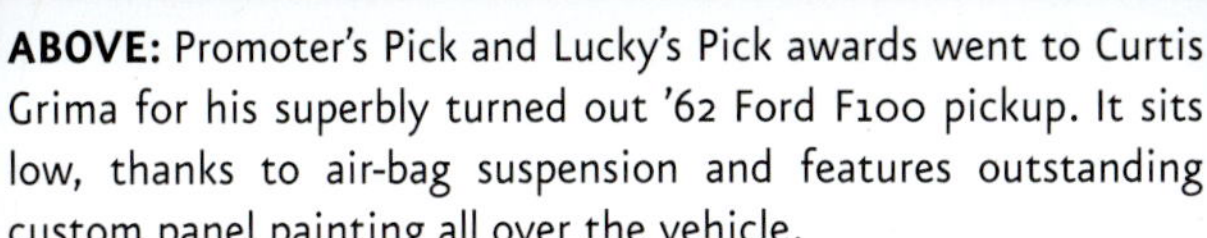

ABOVE: This 1928 Model A Ford Tudor has been chopped four inches, channelled and is fitted with tri-power equipped small block Chevy running gear. It was entered by Ian and Vanessa Wicks and features green leather interior trim with a 1940 Ford steering wheel. The purple tunnel ram 350 Chev motivated T bucket alongside belongs to Old Time Street Rod Club member, Darren Abela.

DLRA SPEED WEEK
LAKE GAIRDNER — SOUTH AUSTRALIA

Early reports prior to Speed Week 2021 indicated good salt with some dampness at the lake access point. The road in from Iron Knob was generally in good condition with just the odd spot where caution needed to be exercised not to enter the water crossings too fast. However, the access road to the lake itself had one really bad patch of bulldust that tested your driving skills to enable safe transition across this section. At times traversing this piece of road was somewhat like driving a boat through rough water except that the waves coming over the bow were made of talcum-powder-like bulldust. One motorcycle rider even fell and hurt himself badly enough to need medical attention.

Arrival at the lake edge on Monday morning saw things progressing smoothly and everyone obeying the request to drive onto the lake very carefully so as not to dislodge the mats that protect the damp surface in this area. It held up very well for the first part of the week and even survived the downpour of rain on Wednesday. Once out on the surface proper it was immediately apparent that the salt was in excellent condition, quite dry and very smooth.

Racing started right on time on Monday morning and the DLRA did an excellent job of keeping it running like clockwork all day long. In fact, this was the most successful first day of racing ever with 235 runs being made on the two courses for the day. The previous record was 190 runs. Delays were absolutely minimal with an hour long lunch break in the middle of the day.

Weather conditions were near perfect with a cool breeze keeping the heat at bay for most of the day. Occasionally the breeze strengthened, giving some of the drivers of high speed cars concern about cross winds down the track. Several new entries were obvious amongst the regulars and everyone was in an upbeat mood, glad to be back racing on Lake Gairdner after a two year COVID induced break.

While racing was continuous and most teams were running very well, not a lot of new record speeds were set. One exception was Gemma Dunn in the family lakester, setting a new record for her class at 215.382 mph. Things took a step up on the Tuesday when several new records were set and the Barnes lakester put down an impressive 275 mph run with its big Ford engine sounding very strong and more left in it.

A new feature of Speed Week Speed 2021 was a junior racers section where kids as young as 11 were able to race a lakester and motorcycles on the short track in their own allotted time. Several competitors took advantage of this new class and it was carried off very successfully.

Words & Photos: Larry O'Toole

TOP: The red Falcon ute of Jeffrey and Luke Haley used a 406 cubic inch Cleveland to post a best speed of 178.453 mph with Jeffrey driving, but Luke got to set a record for B/FALTU at 177.884 mph.

TOP RIGHT: The meeting director on his tower, Steve Charlton does a stirling job of making sure everything runs to schedule and that all rules are obeyed.

ABOVE: A wild spin didn't stop Tom Noack getting with the program and setting a new 209.919 mph record in C/GCC class.

ABOVE RIGHT: Nerve centre for the Speed Week is the control caravan in the pits where DLRA president, Greg Wapling and Secretary/Treasurer Carol Hadfield keep tabs on all the operational facets of Speed Week.

MAIN & ABOVE CENTRE: King of Lake Gairdner for 2021 was Eddie Zeller, making the fastest run of the meet at 275.149 mph in the Barnes bellytank.

ABOVE LEFT: All that cowling work on the bonnet of this Escort is to accommodate a Falcon Barra engine in the engine bay.

ABOVE: Sleek looking lakester was entered by South Australian veteran hot rodder and drag racer, Serge Bonetti.

ABOVE: The Black Ice Racing Team fielded three bikes and are veterans of the Lake Gairdner event.

RIGHT: Junior racers had their own session this year in the "Childs Play" lakester and on motorcycles. Tucked the lakester is a happy 11 year old Kylie Gray.

LEFT: Yes, it's a desirable supercharged Vincent engine powering this APS bike entered by Stuart Penn that made a fastest run of 98.814 mph.

BELOW: So efficient and trouble free was the racing right from the start on Monday that by 11:00am the start line of Number 1 track looked like this! Not a race car in sight and the start line staff with time to have a catch-up.

DLRA SPEED WEEK

ABOVE: Best speed this year for the popular Terraplane from WA was an impressive 200.879 mph qualifier by Darren Banks before the rain. Nothing quite matches the sound of the ugly old thirties era sedan booming across the salt on a high speed run.

In all the years I have been coming to Lake Gairdner for Speed Week I can't recall a more successful two days of racing. It was continuous with minimal downtime, only one major engine blow-up that I heard about and one high speed spin out, most likely as a result of a wind gust as the Long Shot Commodore was entering the timing area. The car came to a stop after several long spins and remained on its wheels with no major damage done.

Having photographed everything extensively over these two days it was time for us to head for home so we left early on the Wednesday

BELOW: Only the second time out for Kym Debrenni's G/BGMR 1934 Ford Roadster "DLRA Salt Dancer" and he only made on pass before selling the car to a new owner on the spot. Kym hasn't left salt lake racing, he's already well under way with a new competition vehicle.

morning with the skies looking threatening with dark rain clouds. Sure enough we encountered quite a bit of rain on the way out and held concerns for how much more racing they would be able to achieve. Once back into normal communications near Port Augusta we saw an image from the lake showing the pits very wet with water from significant rainfall. Our worst fears had been realised, but with those two fantastic days of racing already completed the early interruption of Speed Week didn't detract from it being a most successful event.

ABOVE: The planned all-female racing team of Gemma Dunn and Rachelle Splatt didn't eventuate in 2020 but they did it in 2021. Above Gemma looks serious while listening to dad Mark, before making her first runs. She needn't have been concerned, she set a new C/GL record at 215.382. Above left we have crew members getting Gemma ready for her first run and pushing the lakester to the start line.

ABOVE & BELOW: At top left is the potent engine of the Dunn lakester, no not some blown monster, just a very well prepared and obviously powerful small block Chevy. Crew members push the lakester forward for Rachelle Splatt to make her first ever run on the salt, also a little pensive at first, but she needn't have worried either, completing two successful licensing runs before the rain stopped proceeedings. Rachelle's best run was 208.558 mph.

MAIN & LEFT: Wombat Racing team of David Bullock and Peter Taylor are obviously long time supporters of the Lake Gairdner event as you can see by the number of tech inspection "checked" stickers on the cowling of their lakester. Best speed this year was 216.229 mph by David, while Peter's best was 198.339 mph.

BELOW: It was a frantic Speed Week from start to finish for Peter Max with his V12 Mercedes racer (see separate story starting on page 184). He'll be back in the future with the experience under his belt, ready for another assault on the salt.

ABOVE: Nifty little bike of Malcolm Hewett runs in A/VG using a 1350cc 1950 Vincent engine to run a best speed at the 2021 Speed Week of 139.212 mph.

LEFT: A more serious looking machine is Stuart Hooper's 1959 Velocetette that pumped out a best speed of 182.177 mph.

DLRA SPEED WEEK

MAIN AND BELOW: V8 power pushed the 2003 Bullet SS roadster of Blake Clare to a new record of 205.553 mph.

BELOW: Also setting a new record was Aaron Crocker on his MPS-PG 1650 2004 Harley Davidson at 148.487 mph.

ABOVE: No official speed was recorded for Andrew Butcher on his MBVG-500 1925 Triumph, indicating he never completed a successful run.

ABOVE: Rob Carroll has been punting his six cylinder powered 1997 Falcon in E/GALT class for a number of years and went close to his best with a 165.045 mph speed on this occasion. Dry Lakes racing doesn't have to be expensive!

LEFT & BELOW: Smooth, tapered fairing on Chris Cameron's APS75 OBF 2009 Honda accentuates its length. Top speed for the sleek looking Honda was 119.004 mph.

RIGHT: Steve Morgan and John Viles almost wore the 1984 Toyota ute out, consistently breaking their own records on successive runs until Steve finally nailed it at 165.824 mph, just 0.261 better than John's average.

ABOVE: You learn to expect the unexpected at Lake Gairdner, so it is only a little surprising that an original 1927 Chevrolet tourer would brave the dusty road in from Iron Knob.

RIGHT: Russell Lowe's LS V8 Chevy powered motorcycle sits at the starting line, almost ready to make another run. Fastest speed was 189.916 mph.

LEFT: Transport around the pits and back and forth to the start line takes many forms but this trio opted for their own custom bicycles as a substitute for walking all that distance.

ABOVE: The black 2005 Falcon ute of Adrian Reid went successively faster on each run until he put down a best speed of 223.780 mph before the rain.

DLRA SPEED WEEK

LEFT: Phil Cvirn prepares to leave his crutches behind and climb aboard his MPS/PF 1650 1964 Harley Davidson that turned a best speed of 142.626 mph.

BELOW: Nobody made more runs than Rob Waters in the beautiful Kenworth truck. He made eight runs before the rain set in on Wednesday morning. Beginning with speeds around 122 mph, he eventually pushed it all the way up to a new record 141.314 mph, leaving a trail of smoke across the salt lake on each run.

TOP: Not many dry lakes racers run on straight LPG, but Alan Lacey's 1989 Ford Panel Van does with a best speed of 108.711 mph for the 2021 meet.
ABOVE: Andrew Hutchinson built his Model A coupe for the street, but decided he would give it a couple of meets on the lake first. Some work was needed to pass scrutineering, but he got to make one run at 93.650 mph.

BELOW: The Moe Boys Falcon set a new record in A/CPRO class with a 208.426 mph run with David Nicholson at the wheel.

TOP: Bob Bowman's Cleveland-powered T roadster that runs in D/GMR has been a veteran of the DLRA Speed Week for many years and was sold during this year's event as a going concern, incluidng the venerable converted bus transporter. Trevor May drove it this year, but no speed was recorded.

ABOVE: Ian Robinson's black Pontiac Trans Am was a new entry for 2021 running in AA/GC class, but a speed of only 72.305 mph indicates that all did not go well. He'll be back for another try.

TOP: Norm Hardinge and Neil Davis only got to make one run each this year before the diff ate some teeth on Neil's 169.681 mph run, stopping any further racing for this year.

ABOVE: Low profile streamliner of Danny Plecas prepares to make a pass with some of the bodywork left in the pits, went fastest at 150.890 mph.

TOP: Russell Lowe perches in front of the V8 engine in his APS-5000 motorcycle that managed a best speed of 189.916 mph.

ABOVE: Gene Lopeman's outfit is a pristine 1957 Sporton HD that he rode to 87.419 mph on the almost perfect Lake Gairdner salt.

DLRA SPEED WEEK

MAIN: The Bradshaw Taxi made several strong runs and here it heads for the start line in preparation for yet another attempt to break a record.

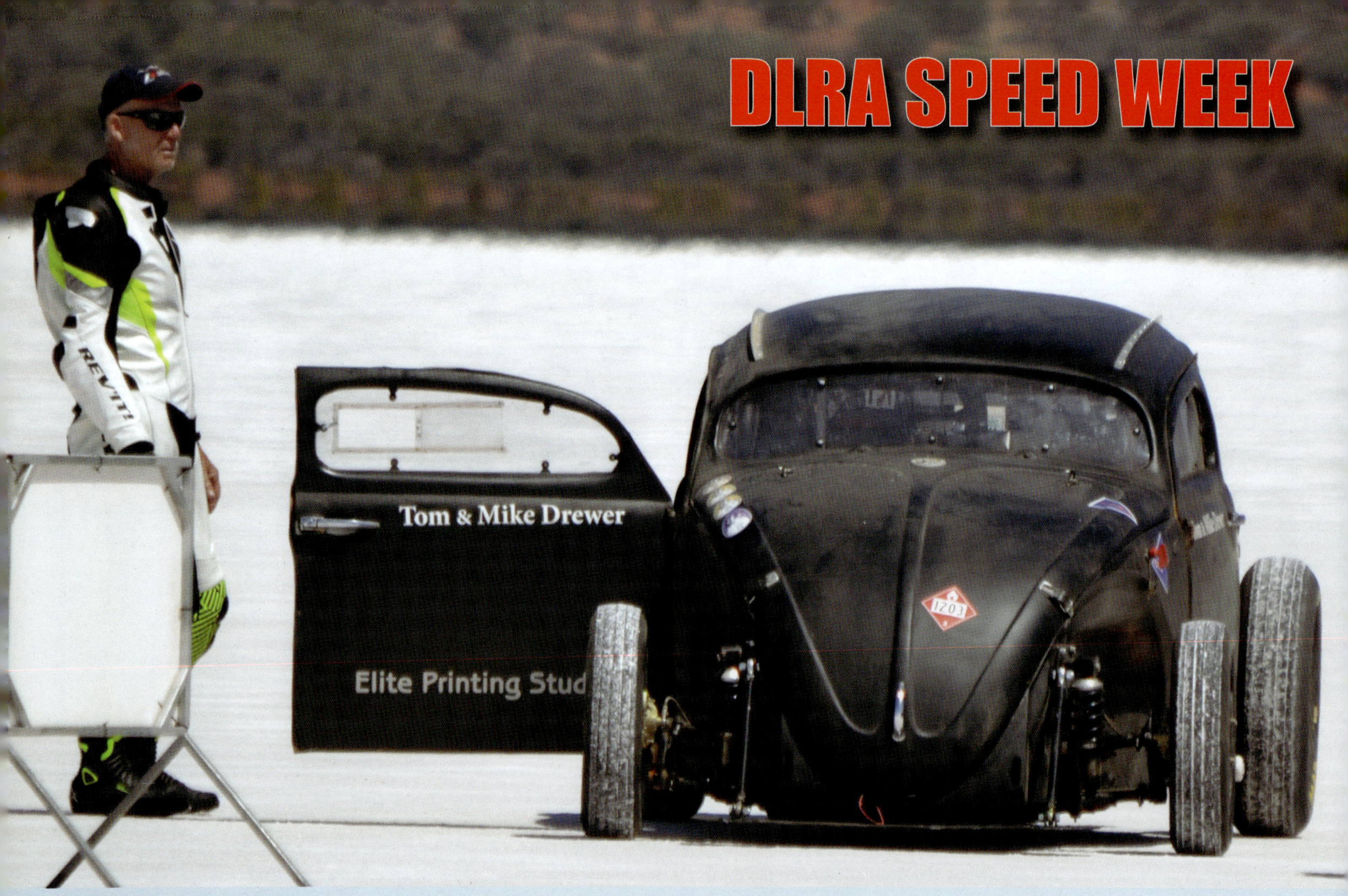

ABOVE: Tom and Mike Drewer's 1964 Volkswagen is a regular at Speed Week and went 160.401 mph with Mike in charge this time.

LEFT: Gnome Racing Commodore is a little different in that it runs a stout Chevy six cylinder engine that powered Graham Cain to 163.466 mph.

BELOW LEFT: Scott Pierce's 2000 Commodore Auscar was one of two such NASCAR based vehicles running this year. After several runs the best speed for Scott was 149.430 mph.

BELOW: Perch on a motorcycle and go as fast as you can. That's what Simon Hills did on his 250 Yamaha that topped out at 117.843 mph.

ABOVE: Paul Teelow heads off on his 2008 Harley Davidson that netted a fastest run of 146.381 mph.
LEFT: Greg Telford's 2015 Special XO BGL lakester put down a fastest run of 142.273 mph.

ABOVE LEFT: A big adventure for Kevin Johns and his daughter Melissa as they braved the road into the salt lake in Kevin's 1927 T.

ABOVE: Jeffery Jones is another competitor that has been to Lake Gairdner many times and improving his top speed each time. This year he went 161.732 mph in his 1981 Corolla that runs in E/BFCC class.

LEFT & BELOW: Long Shot Racing were running strong in the C/GCC 1993 Holden VP Commodore and Tom Noack broke their personal record with a 209.919 average run, despite spinning out on a previous attempt.

TOP: Pontiac Firebird based NASCAR was entered by Ian Robinson, but only made one unsuccessful run before the big rain storm stopped play.

ABOVE: The Taxi really hit full song this year with several 250+ mph runs and a best of 264.464 mph. Kevin Geoffrey earned himself a 200mph Achievers Award in the car as well with a 204.637 mph pass.

LEFT: Matthew Saunders has been a salt lake stalwart for many years so this time he let daughter Heidi make most of the runs in the 253 Holden V8 powered Fiat Topolino. Best speed was 140.630 mph.

NEW Records DLRA Speed Week 2021

252	Stephen Morgan	1984 Toyota	D/MMP	165.824 mph
322	Greg White	1998 AU Falcon	B/BFCC	256.464 mph
389	Ben James	1972 Kawasaki 900	1650 A-CG	153.515 mph
522	Blake Clare	2003 Bullet SS Rdstr	E/BGMS	205.553 mph
612	John Ladbrook Snr	2003 Suzuki GSXR	500 MPS/BF	162.202 mph
735	Paul Powditch	2008 Suzuki	750 P/P	177.076 mph
783	Ken Robinson	1989 Suzuki	500 A/BF	144.583 mph
801	David Nicholson	1973 XA Ford Coupe	A/CPRO	206.426 mph
889	Steven Kell	2003 Suzuki	750 A/G	164.805 mph
913	Peter Curran	1988 Honda	250 M/F	92.570 mph
933	Paul Marcos	2003 Suzuki	650 M/G	150.091 mph
978	Paul Wilkins	1955 Jawa 175	M/VG	71.088 mph
034	Tom Noach	1993 VP Commodore	C/GCC	209.919 mph
1149	Gemma Dunn	2012 Special Const	C/GL	215.382 mph
1171	Arthur DeMain	1988 Toyota	E2/E	103.787 mph
1218	Jean-Paul Afflick	2021 Afflick	100 APS/BF	131.228 mph
91218	Jean-Paul Afflick	2020 Bidalot	50 APS/F	96.875 mph
1228	Tony Brearley	1970 Special Constr	500 A/CF	127.065 mph
1271	Martin Hobson	1982 Triumph	750 MPS/PF	134.292 mph
1283	Paul Mcleod	2014 Bones	175 A/G	109.946 mph
1291	Martin Powditch	2004 Suzuki	650 APS/F	170.017 mph
1335	Aaron Crocker	2004 Harley Davidson	1650 MPS/PG	148.487 mph
1393	Nikki Brearley	1987 Special Const	250 A/G	97.089 mph
1426	Rob Waters	2016 Kenworth	AA MDT	141.314 mph
1447	Steven McGrath	2017 Custom Made	650 A/F	160.359 mph
1475	Jeffrey Solomano	1968 Sprite 250	A/CG	73.376 mph
1475	Jeffrey Solomano	Kawasaki Green	125 MPS/F	89.679 mph

NEW Records DLRA Speed Week 2021 (continued)

1505	Cliff Stovall	2016 Harley	2000 M/PG	160.517 mph
1566	Benjamin Versteegh	1957 Velocette	500 MPS/PG	91.508 mph
1566	Benjamin Versteegh	1980 BMW	650 MPS/PF	106.859 mph
1579	Shane Wilcox	1980 Honda	100 APS/G	100.696 mph
1599	Carlyle Bennett	1980 Honda	100 M/CG	93.724 mph
1624	Luke Haley	1996 XH Ford Ute	B FALTU	177.884 mph
1630	Robert Mason	1981 Honda	250 M/CG	84.346 mph
1637	Paul Treelow	2008 Harley Davidson	1650 MPS/PBG	145.840 mph
1669	Charlie Hallam	2019 Royal Enfield	650 M/F	129.569 mph
1671	Brian Wood	2006 Harley Davidson	1650 M/PG	159.801 mph
1678	Simon Hills	1988 Yamaha	250 M/F	116.031 mph
1683	Mason Wakeman	1994 Kawasaki	100 P/P	74.715 mph
1724	Linton Cox	1982 KTM	500 P/PC	95.171 mph

200 MPH CLUB

To be eligible for the 200 mph Club the competitor must have exceeded 200 mph whilst setting a new record for their class.

522	Blake Clare,	Bullet roadster	E/BGMS	205.553 mph
801	David Nicholson,	XA Falcon coupe	A/CPRO	206.426 mph

200 MPH ACHIEVERS

The DLRA also wishes to recognize each of those competitors who have achieved 200 mph for the first time.

983	Kevin Geoffrey	B/BFCC	204.637 mph
1382	Darren Banks	B/BCBFALT	200.879 mph
1639	Rachelle Splatt	C/FL	208.558 mph

Top Speed of the Meet

1585	Eddie Zeller	Bellytank Lakester	275.149 mph

MAIN: The Rabold/Dare lakester moves away from the start line for another run. The team also won the GRAC Monitor's Choice award for 2021. Not everything went to plan, but a speed of 157.264 mph was posted with Michael Dare doing the driving.

LEFT: Tim Guiness entered his yellow 1975 Alfasud Sprint and managed to pump out a speed of 125.865 mph.

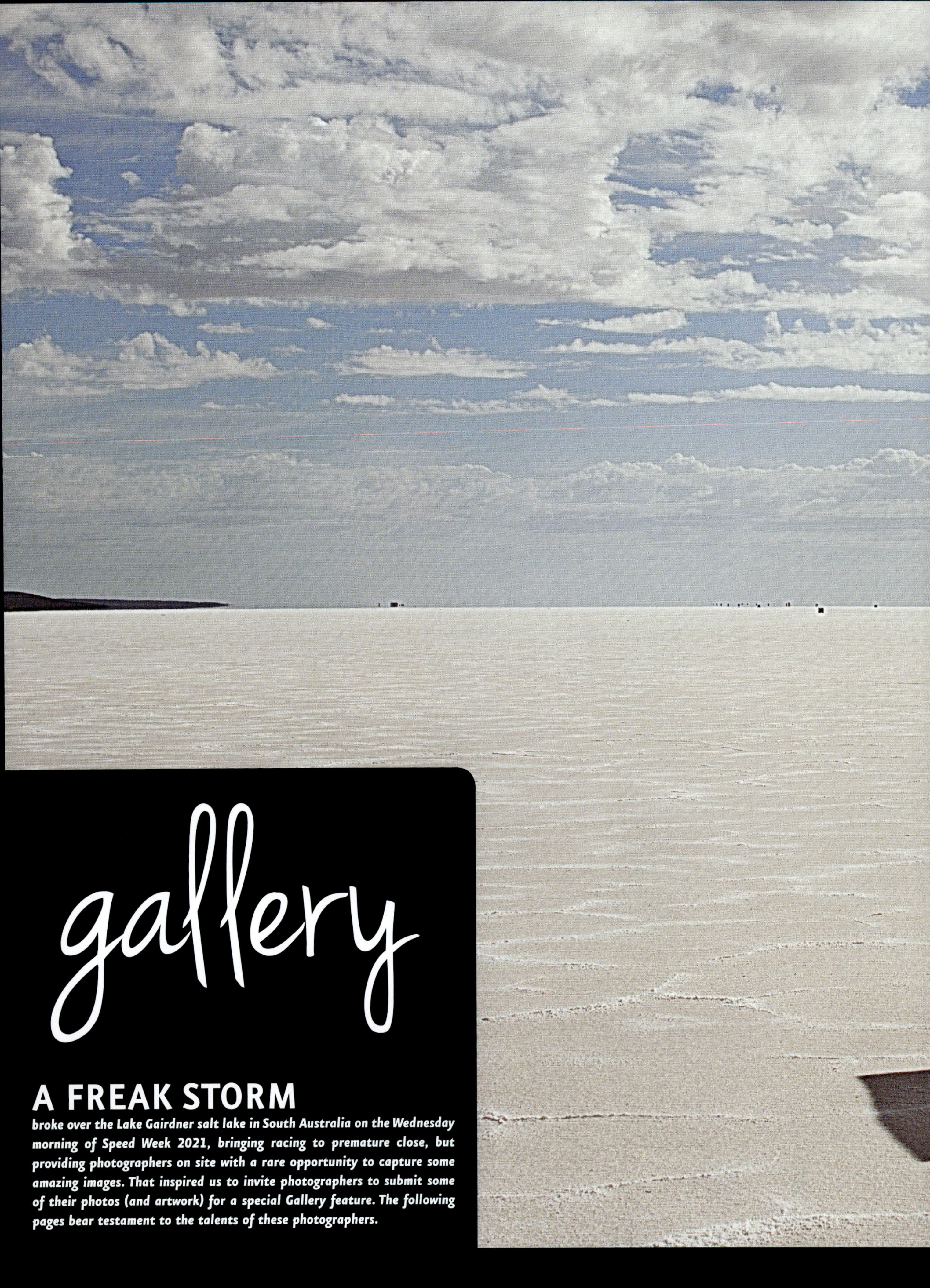

gallery

A FREAK STORM

broke over the Lake Gairdner salt lake in South Australia on the Wednesday morning of Speed Week 2021, bringing racing to premature close, but providing photographers on site with a rare opportunity to capture some amazing images. That inspired us to invite photographers to submit some of their photos (and artwork) for a special Gallery feature. The following pages bear testament to the talents of these photographers.

DLRA SPEED WEEK
gallery
BRETT BOARDMAN

DLRA SPEED WEEK
gallery
MICHELLE PAUL

DLRA SPEED WEEK
gallery
MICHELLE PAUL

JEFF LEMON
SHOEI
S.C.T.A.
BONNEVILLE 2012 NATIONALS
BONNEVILLE 2013 NATIONALS
RED LINE
kawasaki

DLRA SPEED WEEK
gallery
MICHELLE PAUL

DLRA SPEED WEEK
gallery
MICHELLE PAUL

SteveBrown ©2021

DLRA SPEED WEEK
gallery
STEVE BROWN

77
BULLET
Brown ©2021

LONGSHOT

The Stans
DO NOT

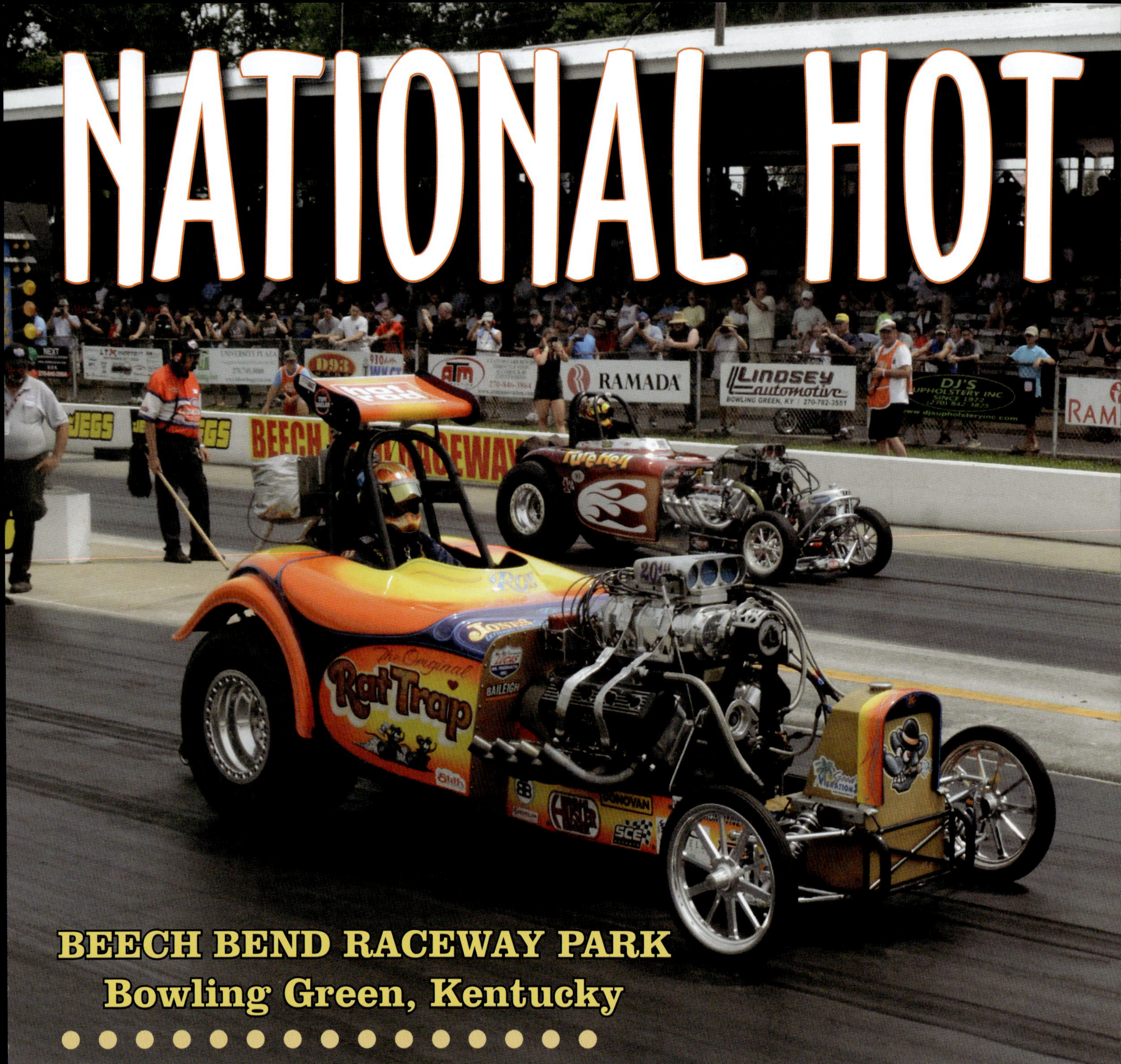

NATIONAL HOT

BEECH BEND RACEWAY PARK
Bowling Green, Kentucky

ABOVE: Fierce competitors and drag racing legends, The Rat Trap takes on Pure Hell in the semi-final round. The Rat Trap prevailed after Pure Hell got a bit out of shape.

LEFT: Jim Murphy heats the slicks up on elimination day prior to taking on Jim Young in the Young Guns rail. Young would get there first and go on to win top fuel title at the 2021 NHRA HRR. Competitive top fuel times were in the fives with speeds above 250 mph.

RIGHT: After the racing and prior to the Cacklefest the winners from the rod run made a parade lap down the side of the track. This burgundy A-V8 roadster is clean and simple, a combination that works every time.

ROD REUNION

**STORY & PHOTOS BY
GERRY BURGER**

ROCKETING INTO THE PAST

Some things never change, and we don't offer that as a complaint. In our rapidly evolving world, with bored billionaires rocketing into space, we discovered a form of time travel right here in Bowling Green, Kentucky. This time travel comes complete with a special brand of rocket-like launches. Thanks to an event produced by the Wally Parks NHRA Museum, (with the tireless museum curator, historian and all-around hot rodder Greg Sharp leading the charge) we have been able to time travel back to the golden age of hot rodding. None of this could happen without the sponsorship of AAA and Holley Performance Products along with the perfect "launch pad" located at Beech Bend Raceway Park.

While the post WWII era is a remarkable time in hot rod history, for many early "boomers", the fifties, sixties and seventies were the golden age of hot rodding. Under the giant umbrella of hot rodding, drag racing became a legitimate motorsport, muscle cars flooded show room floors, and street rodding experienced remarkable growth. The NHRA Holley Hot Rod Reunion is simply a three day celebration of that vintage hot rod culture.

Honestly just rolling into Beech Bend Raceway Park is like stepping back in time. Located on the Barren River among a grove of Beech trees, the scenic park has been entertaining families since the late 1800s. In the 1940s Charles Garvin added pony rides, a roller rink and bowling, along with a swimming pool. Shortly after WWII a 3/8-mile (600m) oval dirt track was added and the in 1956 the drag strip opened. The strip was originally a dirt track, a fairly common racing format in the Southeast. Many old tracks consisted of a paved starting pad that transitioned to dirt, making for some exciting racing.

By the sixties the track was fully paved, had permanent safety walls and held successful races every weekend, along with national caliber events. In the eighties Dallas and Afreda Jones purchased both the drag strip and the oval track and instantly began improvements. The oval went from dirt to pavement, and the drag strip saw an improved track surface and the now iconic chair back, covered grandstands. The seats were removed from a minor league baseball stadium in Nashville, Tennessee in the mid -sixties. This seating is unique for a dragstrip, and some sixty-five years later, the seats contribute greatly to the nostalgic atmosphere that is Beech Bend Raceway Park. Over the years the track has continued to be improved with periodical track resurfacing and paved pit areas, but through it all we are pleased to say "the more things changed, the more they stayed the same", somehow, they managed to make a

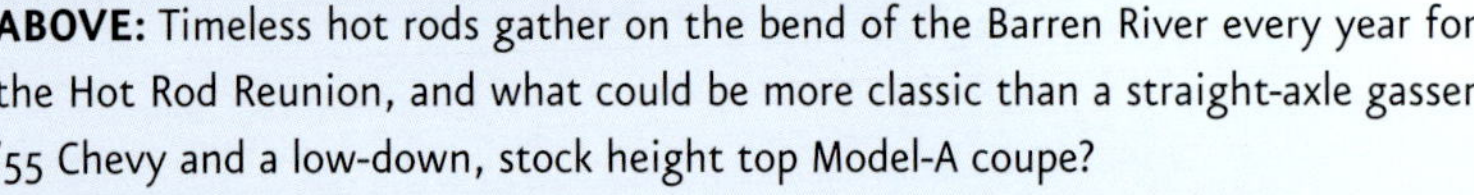

ABOVE: Timeless hot rods gather on the bend of the Barren River every year for the Hot Rod Reunion, and what could be more classic than a straight-axle gasser '55 Chevy and a low-down, stock height top Model-A coupe?

ABOVE RIGHT: Drag racing's winning combination, small car and big motor. With a 327 under the MG bonnet (hoods are for us Yanks) and all four wheels protruding, this is very typical of early gassers. The car appears to be an original survivor.

ABOVE: Scott Rods is home to a group of A/GS cars from the sixties and while this "Cosmic Ray" Corvette was not racing this weekend that blown big block is surrounded by some of the most brilliant metalflake paint on the planet.

LEFT: From flake to candy, this hammered and candy-coated red coupe is powered by a 409 (dipstick on the passenger side, but then you knew that) fed by six-Deuces. White firewall, King Bees and wide whites complete this Hilton Hot Rods built Deuce.

BELOW INSET: Creativity was everywhere, including pit wagons like this one. We have no idea what actually powers this thing but the driver is definitely having fun and he's turning heads.

BELOW: I can think of no better method of time travel than wrapping yourself in red leather and flippin' your fins to the wind in a big old '59 Buick. As the space age dawned the rocket influence was obvious from the fins and taillights to the decklid emblem. Perfect stance and wheels complete the image.

LEFT: This is the very definition of your basic hot rod. Strip the fenders, add juice brakes to the stock axle put a set of big 'n' little wire wheels for a proper rubber rake. Paint is for later, primer works for now.

BELOW LEFT: The Dorman & Koopman AA/SR was built in the mid-sixties to a very high standard, making this both a show and go hot rod. The car is powered by a blown and injected 392-inch Hemi. Chrome suspension, firewall, engine components and tall roll bar all add show points. The car appeared in the January 1966 Car Craft Magazine.

modern racetrack without losing the heritage of the venue. Old race tracks talk to you, and this one has some great stories to tell.

Once again, our time travel is smoother than a rocket launch, just watch about 1000 hot rods stream into the show field, while listening to delighted screams emanating from the wooden roller coaster in the adjoining amusement park.

Traditional events attract "real hot rodders" and their traditional hot rods. The Hot Rod Reunion show field is filled with street going gassers, traditional hot rods, muscle cars and cool trucks. This year the weather was picture-perfect for all three days meaning the drag racing was virtually non-stop. From gassers and pro-stock entries to a full field of front-engine, top fuel dragsters and altereds, it is easy to settle into the sights and sounds of drag racing. Nothing clears the mind (and the sinuses) quite like a snoot full of spent nitromethane.

The Hot Rod Reunion swap meet never disappoints, if you're looking for quilts and homemade jam you probably will be disappointed, but if it is genuine vintage speed equipment and vintage parts you're searching for, this area will deliver hours of shopping.

Since the event is traditionally held on Father's Day weekend it begins on Thursday with final eliminations run on Saturday. As the sun settles behind the Kentucky hills, the top fuel final signals the end of the race weekend, but don't leave just yet.

Next, the show winners from the rod run side make a parade pass down the storied track prior to the big Cacklefest. As darkness creeps in, the "cackle cars" roll into place. Nitro-burning cars ranging from top fuel dragsters to competition coupes and altereds line both sides of the track facing the grandstands. The push-start cars are pushed up the track where they turn around and rumble into the Cacklefest. Many of the push vehicles are as colorful as the dragsters they push. The mechanical-start engines roar to life, flames and fumes fill the air along with a noise like no other. And then, as the glow of the zoomie headers dim, the 18th Wally Parks NHRA Motorsports Hot Rod Reunion is in the books.

This is an event put on by real hot rodders for real hot rodders. If you have a bucket list, this event should be on it and the fact that all proceeds of the Reunion directly support the programs and activities of the Wally Parks NHRA Motorsports Museum gives the event purpose.

We're looking forward to the 2022 NHRA Holley Hot Rod Reunion, for more time travel with old friends, vintage cars, and to enjoy the best nostalgia drag racing on the planet. We hope to see you there, space jockey billionaires need not apply. ■

ABOVE LEFT: The Illinois Outlaw has been making eight-second passes for several years now and the nostalgia style drag car is sure fun to watch. But before the Fiat fun you have to wait your turn in the staging lanes.

LEFT: Nothing looks lower than a stock height top on a channeled A-coupe. Up front a dropped axle is mounted suicide fashion while we're guessing there are some air bags out back. Judging by the blocked off headers this one makes some noise.

NATIONAL HOT ROD REUNION

RIGHT: Drag racing royalty abounds at the HRR. Say the word Fuel Altered and Nanook instantly comes to mind. Dave and Linda Hough have been racing these wildly entertaining Nanook roadsters since the '60s, today, three generations of the Hough family campaign this AA/FA. Dave, Linda, Brian and Kyle Hough still know how to bring the crowd to their feet.

BELOW: Verde Racing took 468-inches of Chevy big block, feed it with a Hilborn mechanical injection and then stuffed it in a lightweight 1948 Austin shell. A true homebuilt car the all-steel Austin runs hard.

ABOVE: Comp coupes were one of the wilder classes in the '50s and '60s. Basically, take a vintage body and make it fit a dragster chassis and you had a Comp Coupe. The Time Traveler is a fine example of the breed, running injected small block Chevy power.

BELOW: Mike Kalinowski drives the "rat infested" Austin known as Unfinished Business. Running with the Scotts Rods gasser group the Angry Austin "wrinkles 'em up" with a typical hard launch.

ABOVE: When it comes to wheel stands nobody does it better than Mike Bilina and his '56 Chevy. Wheel stands, dry hops, burnouts and mid-tens make this '56 Chevy a crowd pleaser. What makes it even better is the car was built in 1965 and very little has been changed. Straight axle, a big block Chevy motor (set back) and magnesium wheels are all sixties fare… hey, even the green tinted windows were done back in the day.

BELOW: The legend of the Rat Trap AA/FA continues, over fifty years after the 1969 debut. Unique with independent front suspension, the Ron Green chassis has proven to be straight and quick. Entertainment is provided by Ron Hope as the pilot, Brian Hope does duty as Crew Chief. It is one wildly entertaining race program. Long live fuel altereds.

LEFT Top to Bottom: The Swamp Fox was actually a 1967 homebuilt effort by Mel Hoyh. Starting with an R&B Chassis he covered it in a beautiful aluminum body. This is the original car, painstakingly restored after thirty years of racing in various configurations, today it Cackles and tells stories.

The Huber Special is in position and proving that not all the popping and fire emanates from hemi engines. The huffed small block had a wicked sound and the short rail reminds us why they call these cars "sling shots".

The Hustlers Car Club put on quite a show with the Pesek & Lucas T/F car from the mid-sixties. You know you're Cacklin' right when your zoomies go red.

A fitting end to a great weekend of racing is the Cacklefest. Vintage top fuel cars often pushed into position by equally vintage push cars. Here the Hundley and Boggs AA/FD rolls down track.

MAIN: Lest you think nostalgia drag racing is "exhibition" check out the clocks after Nick Van Horn in the Panic AA/FA faced Randy Bradford in the Bradford's Fiat AA/FD. Bradford's Fiat turned the light on and it brought the crowd to their feet.

RIGHT: It's difficult to cause a distraction in a Cacklefest… but this cool '27 T-roadster did just that, its' dressed flatmotor, early wires, drilled backing plates and a suicide front end are just some of the highlights of this righteous rod.

ABOVE: The early slingshot rails have a charm all their own. Short wheelbase, iron motors, stack injection and a laid down roll bar hoop all wrapped in rudimentary bodywork. And yes, back when the motors were iron and rear wheels were steel.

ABOVE: "Funny car, eliminations to the staging lanes"... Paul Smith's Entertainer 1978 Corvette with John Bodie Smith behind the wheel, went up against Eric Stevens in the Bluegrass Thunder '69 Camaro. The Corvette prevailed, only to go down in a very close final round.

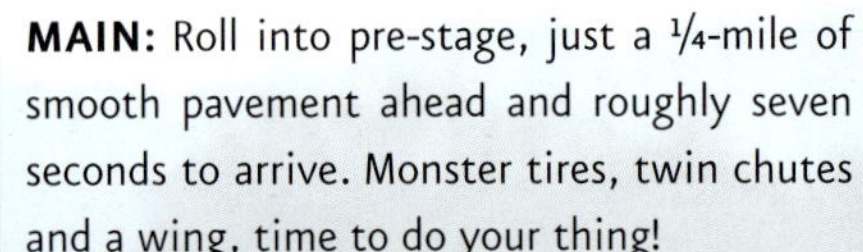

MAIN: Roll into pre-stage, just a ¼-mile of smooth pavement ahead and roughly seven seconds to arrive. Monster tires, twin chutes and a wing, time to do your thing!

ABOVE: Hang around real hot rod events like The NHRA Holley Hot Rod Reunion long enough and you'll find performance literally bursting through hot rod hoods.

ABOVE: This may be the very definition of winning a drag race. The T-shirt tells the story, but watch that senior gentleman with the rule book in his back pocket, ultimately he decides how sketchy things get.

NATIONAL HOT ROD REUNION

TOP: This may be the nicest 1933 Willys rumble seat coupe survivor we've ever seen. Virtually rust free, it still wears a 1951 Kansas license plate. But check out the fit and finish on this car, flawless door gaps and hood fit. Amazing.

ABOVE: The American Graffiti influence is apparent on this '55 Chevy with hood scoop, radiused wheel wells and chrome reverse rims it all adds up to a timeless hot rod. Removing the front bumper on a '55 Chevy was mandatory back in the day, "Falfa" should have.

TOP: If you can still see the rear wheel or tire you're not really doing a burnout, you're just squealing tires. We offer this image of Mike Kalinowski in his Angry Austin to illustrate a "real burnout". The "rat infested' Austin is a fast, fan favorite.

ABOVE: Let's face it, Yanks like their bump stick in the middle, that overhead cam stuff was for exotic cars. But in the sixties Ford came out with the 427 SOHC engine. Originally designed to challenge the Chrysler hemi on circle tracks, the SOHC motor was quickly converted to drag racing. This particular motor once ran in a Jack Nicholson funny car. The Cammer dragster was assembled exclusively to to take part in the Cackle Fest.

BELOW: Super stock and FX cars to the staging lanes, Super Stock… FX cars… to the staging lanes please. The Mopar identity with these classes is dominant.

Alternative Rodding

The Go-Jeep Project

RIGHT: The 1958 Jeep pickup truck in the farmer's paddock. Climbing in and out of a wreck like this as a boy kicked off a desire to one day own one myself and turn it into something special.

BELOW: Body modifications finished and the vehicle basically mocked up around its donor running gear. Unless you knew otherwise it would be hard to pick what is different between this vehicle and the factory produced item.

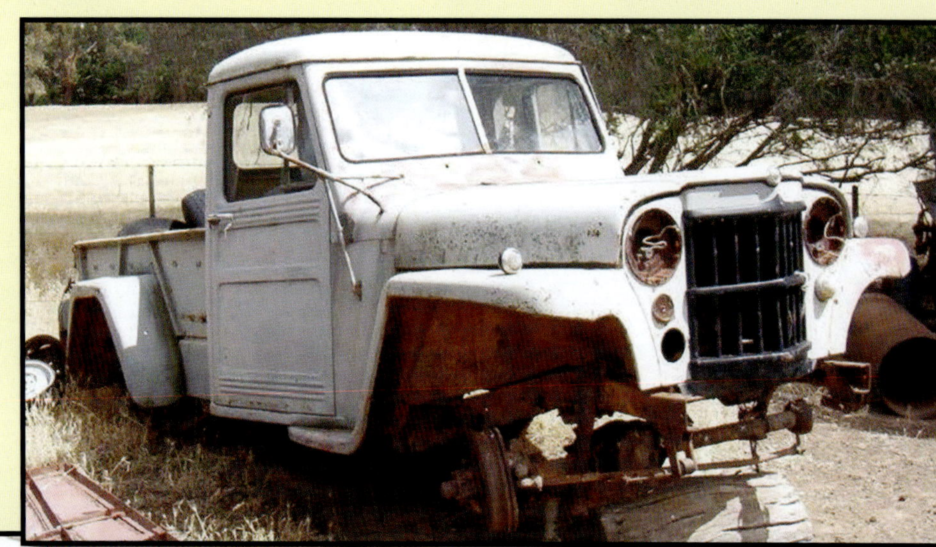

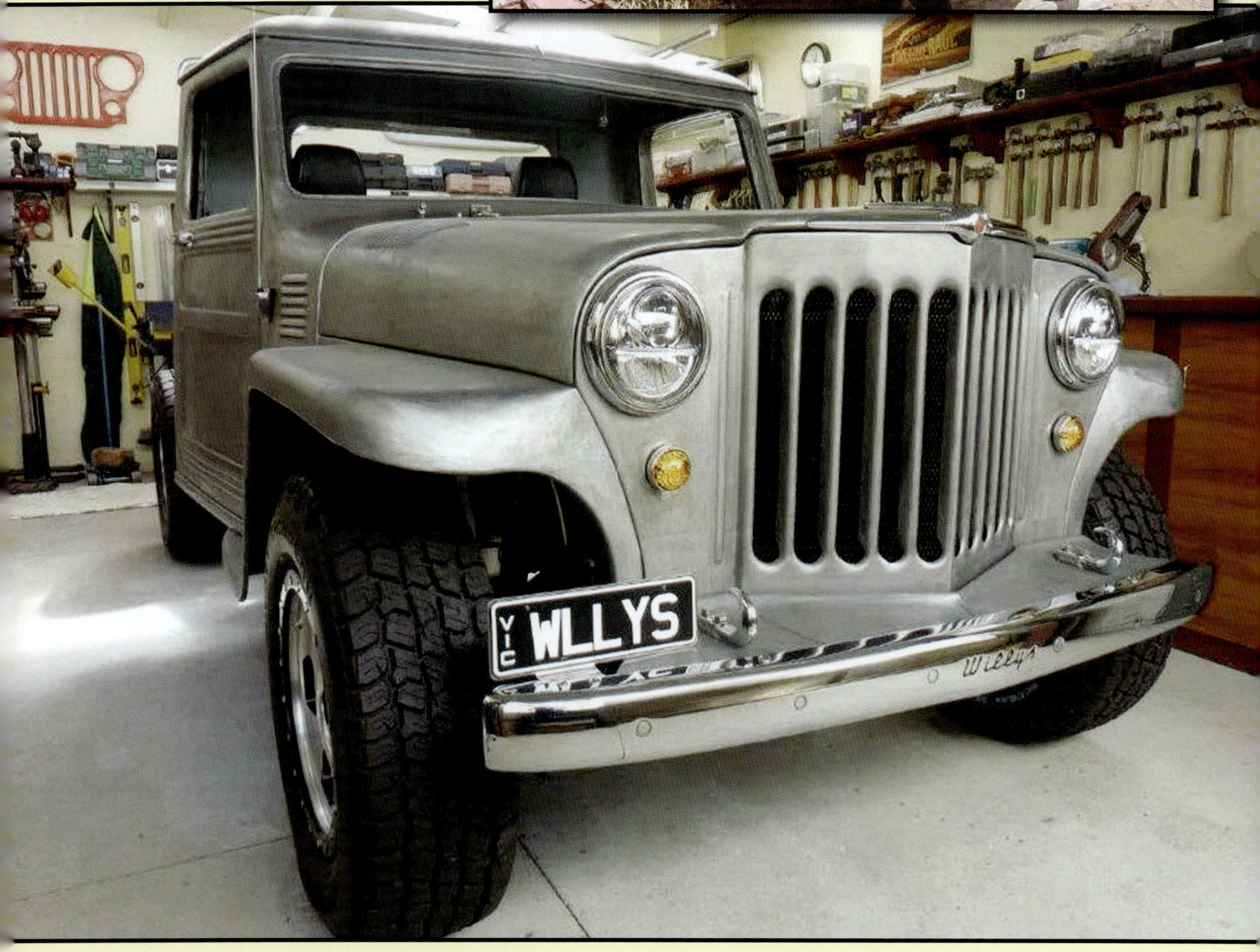

ABOVE: These two become one, 2008 Jeep Grand Cherokee with 5.7 litre V8 Hemi engine was purchased at a Pickles auction in Queensland. The plan was to transplant as much as possible from this wreck into the early pickup alongside.

BELOW: The GEN III Hemi's are still a wide engine! The concept of marrying the two together had people talking. The engine, five speed transmission, transfer case, steering rack, front diff and all the front suspension were successfully fitted into the modified pickup chassis.

This is a long term project to fulfill a childhood dream of building myself a hot rod one day. For some reason I always had in mind a 1950-1964 "pointy nosed" Willys pickup. Maybe that stems back to the time when I would spend my childhood summers down at the beach in San Remo where I would sneak into a nearby yard and climb inside one that was rusting away. I thought of it off and on for years, then one day I saw one come up on eBay, and for a joke, sent the auction details to my wife and mentioned the childhood dream. Instead of thinking it was just folly, she said, "We should bid on it!" Well, we won it and that is how it all started. Mind you, we didn't even have anywhere to put it, but the sellers agreed to keep it in their paddock for me for a few months, that turned out to be nearly a year, until I got my plans through council and then built a small workshop to house it.

The plan was to use a wrecked 2008 Jeep Grand Cherokee with a 5.7 litre V8 Hemi as the main donor and use as much as possible from that vehicle, everything from the whole drive train, including front and rear suspension, the wiring loom and instruments etc. I also planned to widen the cab to cover the donor wheel track and gain much needed room inside the narrow cab and the engine bay. I lengthened the cab as well to gain extra leg room.

The Grand Cherokee was bought on a Queensland Pickles auction site bidding live online. I ended up with the whole vehicle for the same price as just the engine and transmission would normally cost! It was a repairable write off with only 35,000 km on the clock and had only been on the road for a year. I took it for a test drive around the block to make sure everything was working before setting it up dead level in the workshop and spent two weeks photographing and taking data points of every suspension point and its related angles so they could be used on the Willys chassis.

ABOVE: The 1948 Willys Truck frame stripped down to the last bolt and rivet.

ABOVE RIGHT: Frame rail wedge cut out part of the way, and then pressed to increase factory bends.

RIGHT: Chassis and original crossmembers fully boxed and new RHS centre K member and bracing added.

BELOW: First time a rolling chassis.

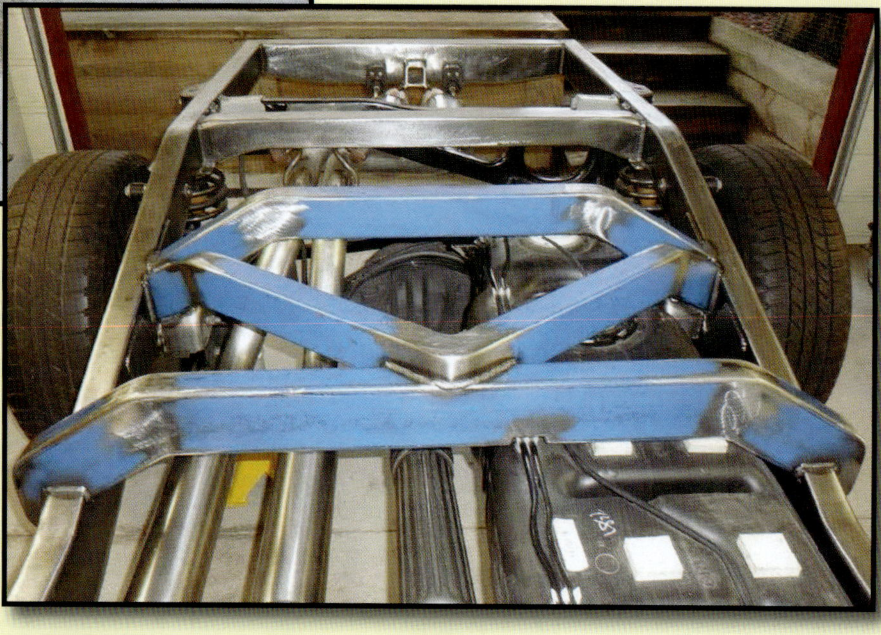

The Go-Jeep Project

The Hemi has twin plugs per cylinder with coils directly on the plugs and features cylinder deactivation, so it will drop to as little as four cylinders in light load conditions. In the end it was easier to drop the front cradle and gearbox crossmember out, complete with the engine, five speed transmission, transfer case, steering rack, front diff and all the front suspension, minus the upper wishbone and coilover mounts, still attached to it. I installed them into the Willys chassis the same way. The main modification was moving the engine mounts back 175mm (7 inches) in the cradle to keep the front axle in the centre of the wheel arch. The front suspension is a double wishbone with coilovers and the rear is a solid axle with 3.73:1 ratio with a five link and coils. The whole unibody frame was carefully removed from the body shell and every mount removed from it including threaded bosses etc that were welded inside.

A second 1948 Willys truck was also purchased to help with the widening and lengthening of the cab. They were branded Willys up until the take over of the Willys Overland company in 1954 by Kaiser, who then dropped the Willys name and referred to them just as Jeeps. It will be registered as a 1948 Willys truck as I am using the 1948 chassis rather than the 1958; it was actually in better condition with less rust. Both chassis' were completely stripped of every crossmember and bracket, so I started with just a pair of bare rails.

To get full suspension travel the same as the donor Jeep, and match up with all of its suspension points, the frame had to be 32mm (1.25 inches) higher at the front and 100mm (4 inches) higher at the rear. This was done by partially cutting a wedge into the back of existing bends in the chassis rail to increase the angle to achieve the required height. The frame rail was never cut all the way through, but stopped 25mm (1 inch) short and then bent in a press to give a smooth rounded bend. The joint was bevelled and fully welded before a fish plate was added on the back of the join to further support it.

Once everything was fitted inside the chassis rails, including threaded bosses and mounts, it was fully boxed with only a single join halfway along. With the boxing plates all tacked into place, the two rails were also tacked to each other, face to face, so all the welding could take place. By carefully balancing the welds in sections, top to bottom and also in the same area on the other rail, it kept everything from warping. A total of 18 metres (59 feet) of welding was done. The rails were then setup on stands and all the bolt-in members from the donor were fitted into place. Next the crossmembers were welded in. The stock Willys crossmembers used were also fully boxed using the same cross member from the 1958 chassis. All the time spent taking notes paid off as the engine, transmission, transfer case, steering rack, lower suspension arms etc. were dropped in once and never taken back out again.

My intention was to build custom stainless steel headers using mandrel bends. But ohaving priced out what I would need, it was far cheaper to buy a set for the 6.1 Hemi SRT Jeeps by OBX. I thought I could modify them to fit where needed and go from there. Well, the only modification needed was making a slot for the EGR port and drilling an extra mounting hole. Even though the port shape is different between the 5.7 and 6.1 Hemis, the larger ports of the 6.1 meant it did not impede exhaust flow at all. Hemis like to breathe and these headers came with 1-7/8 inch primaries that feed into dual three inch collectors. A bonus was that the rest of the system that came with it also fitted up! I only had to swap out the resonators for compliant catalytic converters to suit our emissions requirements.

Having had so much luck with the SRT aftermarket exhaust, I decided to also buy the US dealer optional system from the catalytic converters back, as made by Corsa. It is also fully stainless and runs out to dual centre resonators. This also bolted up remarkably well and I only later changed the layout at the rear, so I could fit a full sized spare between the tailpipes. The donor 80 litre fuel tank was fitted in the same place as stock and then a K member was added to complete the requirements for the chassis. All the right hand side was bent in a similar way

TOP: Hemi headers for a 6.1 Hemi SRT Jeep by OBX were a cheaper option to making them out of stainless steel myself and they only needed very slight modification, a slot for the EGR port and drilling an extra mounting hole. From the end of the headers I was able to use SRT Hemi Corsa stainless steel exhausts from the catalytic converter to the back.

ABOVE: The cab was built from just these little pieces! added to the donor floor pan and firewall.

BELOW: Hand forming new louvres. I made a die by cutting out the perimeter shape of the louvre in some plate and welded a back to it. The sheet metal was clamped down hard and the metal split using an old wood chisel directly over the very edge of the form underneath. The rest of the forming was then done using a piece of red gum shaped to the louvre profile and hammered into the form.

TOP & ABOVE: New roof skin made on an English Wheel and TIG welded into place.

TOP RIGHT: Upper half added with the gap showing the difference in cab width.

ABOVE RIGHT: Mocking up some pieces to start building the cab.

RIGHT: Cab mounted on the rolling chassis.

The Go-Jeep Project

to the chassis with a wedge cut, plus a technique used on the uncut face to give a factory looking radius to the bends.

I started the cab build from the ground up using the donor floor and firewall. This gave me most of the mounts to suit the donor interior hardware. Everything from the seats, hanging pedals, to the air conditioner unit and console etc., already have their mounts in place. From the two cabs I mainly used the lower half from the 1958 and the top half from the 1948 which were the best parts of each. The 1948 cab also had the more desirable small rear window and I made up most of the centre section of the cab so I could gain the extra width I was after. The rest was hand made to fill in the missing sections.

The original top opening cowl vent could not be used, so I had to come up with another way to get fresh air into the donor air conditioner unit. I decided on some louvres on the side of the cowl but couldn't find any to match the ones I wanted to add to the bonnet. So I made a die by cutting out the perimeter shape of the louvre in some plate and welded a back to it. The sheet metal was clamped down hard and the metal split using an old wood chisel directly over the very edge of the form underneath. The rest of the forming was then done using a piece of red gum shaped to the louvre profile and hammered into the form.

The cab length extension was done to get some much-needed legroom and also to help balance the extra width that had been added. Before the donor was stripped down, I adjusted the seat to where it was comfortable for my tall frame, and then ran a plumb bob from behind the head rest to the floor to determine where it needed to be cut. I turned up a flange along the edge of the floor so that the rear wall had a return to suit plug welding. Panels were stripped using a strip disc, repairs done and then soaked in a bath of citric acid to remove all the rust. Subtle changes were made such as extending the bead along the front of the cowl all the way to the bottom and meeting the extended swage of the door sill. An embossed, pressed Willys name was also added to either side of the lower cowl and the panel seam fully welded instead of just spot welded together.

The cab was sectioned by 50mm (two inches) below the rear window. I didn't want the window any smaller as it was already short in height. A laser level was used to set the cut lines so that everything was straight and true. The rear wall ended up needing 265mm (10.5 inches) added to it due to the wedge shape of the cab having been made longer. Pieces were hand formed to match the window profile and fill in the gap.

I was very fortunate to be invited to attend several metal meets. I made profiles of the larger roof skin needed and took the sheet metal with me. Peter Tommasini instructed me on how to get started on wheeling up the panel. I was then able to finish off the wheeling at home to get the exact fit I required. Only parts of the outer edge are from the Willys and they were changed by cutting 50mm (two inches) from them and tipping a new flange to pancake the roof. All the panel welding was done using TIG and planished afterwards to make everything metal finished.

Rather than shortening the height of the windscreen, a 50mm (two inch) section was removed below the opening and the whole screen moved lower. This made it closer in height to the side windows after they were chopped. A new upper section of the firewall was made to join the donor firewall to the Willys cowl. The whole top of the cowl had to be reshaped to flow into the lowered windscreen and also because of the extra width of the cab. The old top cowl vent hole was replaced with a Willys stamped piece from the middle of a 1942 CJ2a Willys tailgate.

The doors were lengthened 115mm (4.5 inches) by using two doors so there was only one seam. The door window frames were shortened by 50mm (two inches) to match the sections taken out of the cab. The B pillars were made 65mm (2.5 inches) wider to complete the 175mm (7 inch) cab extension. Overall from the floor to the centre of the roof is now 100mm (four inches) lower than stock. Doors have already been gapped and no lead was used anywhere on the body.

The window opening is the same height as stock but new pieces were formed to

ABOVE: Shows the difference between the stock bonnet and the custom one. Note the louvres from an FJ45 added to the rear edges of the widened version.

RIGHT: Some of the pieces that made up the new bonnet. The two narrow pieces behind show what was cut out and then replaced with the 115mm (4.5 inches) wider pieces to get the extra width needed. It had to be done this way because extra width was added to the grille either side of the raised centre section.

BELOW: Front view of finished cab with widened grille and bonnet all fitted in place.

The Go-Jeep Project

fill in the gaps left by the cab widening, making the window longer than before. The lower wall has outer sections from the 1958 cab and the centre from the 1948 to make up the extra width.

The bonnet was one of the hardest panels to get perfect as you will always be able to see both sides of the panel. I first removed all the panel damage such as numerous dents etc., then welded in some bonnet vents from a Land Cruiser FJ45. They were badly damaged but I was able to repair them and altered their contour to suit the Willys bonnet. The two narrow pieces behind show what was cut out and then replaced with the 115mm (4.5 inches) wider pieces to get the extra width needed. It had to be done this way because extra width was added to the grille either side of the raised centre section.

As the front V section was made wider, it also became longer as the angles were left stock. The grille was brought forward so the new bonnet ended up 177mm (9 inches) wider and 75mm (3 inches) longer. There was 7.5 metres, (24.5 feet) of welding done and 10 pieces in all just on the skin. It took two weeks of careful TIG welding, planishing and shrinking to get it free of any oil canning and then metal finished.

The grille of the 1948 Willys had 10 narrow slots and the 1958 grille had eight wide slots, so I ended up using all wide slots and adding one more to each side which gave 125mm (5 inches) of extra width. Another 50mm (2 inches) strip of metal was added between the grille slots and the headlights to give the full 127mm (9 inch) width needed. I bead rolled these to give them a factory appearance.

The slotted area now matches the width of the donor radiator core and the tanks tuck in behind the added pieces each side. I found this better looking than just adding the width to the grille slot area, or all between the grille and the headlights.

ABOVE: This is just the interior wiring harness laid out on the floor of the workshop.

RIGHT: 1948 grille top left, 1958 top right and new, widened grille below.

ABOVE: Starting the process of fitting up the donor dash.

BELOW: Close-up view of the upper wishbone and coil-over brace.

The Go-Jeep Project

As the donor firewall was used, the engine fits perfectly in front of it. The distance between the engine and firewall was kept the same as factory. I was even able to plumb the whole Willys using the donor fuel, transmission, air conditioner lines and hoses etc. The donor also provided the radiator and air conditioning condenser that was all engineered to work together. Even the hydraulically driven, ECU speed controlled engine fan was used. The brake booster and master cylinder were mounted straight back onto the firewall exactly the same to operate all the donor brakes including the full ABS system that includes the traction control, electronic stability, brake assist and roll mitigation systems.

The donor was of unibody construction so it relied on the body panels around the engine bay to carry the load on the upper wishbone and coil-over mount. It did have a single cross-over brace for extra support. As the Willys panels are not used at all for support, I added a second cross-over brace and made a tie-in plate to carry the load and therefore stop the chassis rails twisting. Also shown are the early Hemi valve covers that I have modified to use as coil covers, not to make it look like an old Hemi, but to clean up the look of the modern Hemi and give a nod to its heritage. I prefer an engine to still look like an engine, rather than cover it up with a fancy engine cover.

The chassis/driveline wiring was of a similar amount as shown in the picture, but most of it was used. The interior wiring however had to be completely dissected. Wiring for the rear wiper, doors, hatch etc., was not needed. I had to print out 80 pages just to follow where all the wiring for the doors went! The donor was wired using the CANBUS system and there were 28 modules in all. This all works fine if you can actually physically fit the donor components into place, but that is not always possible. Things like the CANBUS controlled wipers wouldn't fit under the cowl, so I adapted the donor motor to drive a new Lucas cable wiper gearbox and the problem was solved. Now the wiper stalk controls, with intermitted speeds etc., will work properly.

As much as possible from the donor will be used inside the cab as the theme is 2008 inside the cab and underneath the vehicle, and 1948 for the exterior body panels. It was a top of the line Limited version with full leather electric adjustable heated seats that bolt straight back into place on the donor floor and plug into the donor harness. It has drive by wire throttle pedal and full satellite navigation with left and right climate controlled A/C. The depth of the dash had to be

shortened a lot but still flows into the base of the windscreen. This was why I sectioned the cab 50mm (two inches) so it would match up.

For rolling stock I had a hard time finding something that fitted the theme of the vehicle and had a suitable offset to suit the modern driveline. In the end I settled on some American Racing AR969 Ansen wheels in 17x8 inches with a +25 offset to match the 5 on 5 inch Jeep stud pattern. For the tyres I wanted an all terrain but without the busy sidewalls. I chose some 265/70R17 (32 x 11 inches), Mickey Thompson Deegan 38s. The side shot also shows the extra 25mm (1 inch) that I lowered the grille to get a nice slope to the bonnet and the grille was moved forward for better clearance in front of the engine. The outside of the guard was left stock and the inside was extended, along with the new inner guards, while the bonnet is 75mm (3 inches) longer than stock overall.

I imported a rear bumper off a same era Willys Wagon that had the Willys script stamped into it and fitted it to the front. Rust and dent repairs were made and then the old front bolt holes were made to accept chrome plated front parking sensors. The bumper was then re-chromed to its former glory, along with the Wagon bonnet ornament. The Narva LED headlights have the full ADR and DOT approvals, and were also fitted to the last series of the Land Rover Defender and to some Kenworth Trucks. Indicators are LED and suit a Land Rover Defender as well.

This project has been 10 years in the making so far, working on it whenever I could. I made sure it always stayed a learning experience, even if it was in patience sometimes! I have always loved working with metal since my high school metal work classes. I have been everything from a blacksmith/farrier to a boiler maker. Working as a brake mechanic for a time also came in handy.

The tray will be completely hand built at home. So far, no work has been farmed out at all, apart from the chrome, but I hope to have it painted professionally in as yet an un-decided colour. This has been the hardest thing to decide on. After much encouragement from others I intend to run it in bare metal for the first summer after the truck is fully engineered and registered.

I would like to give the most thanks to my ever supportive wife who even buys more tools for me, saying I can still use them when I build her hot rod next! I also appreciate the support from family and friends and members on the forums who have encouraged me along the way. ■

LEFT: American Racing wheels with Mickey Thompson tyres are used at front and rear.

BELOW: I imported a rear bumper off a same era Willys Wagon that had the Willys script stamped into it and fitted it to the front.

Music Begets Art

THE JAMES HETFIELD COLLECTION

James Hetfield might be best recognized as the frontman of the band Metallica, but car enthusiasts know him for being a huge custom car collector/builder. James Hetfield amassed a solid collection of custom cars, many built with customizer Rick Dore. Hetfield recently donated some of those customs to the Petersen Museum in Los Angeles, California which subsequently produced the "Reclaimed Rust" exhibit.

Hetfield always had an interest in cars like most youths growing up in the sixties. In an interview with the Petersen Museum, he noted, "I just hung out with guys that had cars" in high school in Downey, California. But he admits "This stuff would not have happened without the brilliant eye and mind of a great friend of mine, Rick Dore. Rick Dore's influence, walking me through a lot of the car shows... allowed me to get to the next level. We were able to hook up and join forces and create some art that nobody had done before."

The display featured ten cars, six of which were produced with Rick Dore. The Petersen Museum intends on now loaning the exhibit out to other sites so others can appreciate these rolling pieces of art. As the exhibit was winding down, Dore took time to give Hot Rodding International an inside look at how these cars came to be.

Dore stated the friendship with Hetfield started nearly twenty years ago. Hetfield had known about Rick Dore and his custom cars. At a Mooneyes Show in California, Hetfield came up and introduced himself and commented how much he liked Dore's work. Later a tattoo artist, Corey Miller, introduced Hetfield to more of the custom car culture and Hetfield then joined the Beatniks car club that Dore also belonged to.

Hetfield later invited Dore to Las Vegas, Nevada for a concert. At that time Hetfield mentioned he was buying online a 1953 Buick Skylark to be customized. A year later while at Hetfield's garage, which he called "The

ABOVE: Petersen Museum Executive Director Terry L. Karges conducts a live interview session with James Hetfield during the official opening of the "Reclaimed Rust" exhibition.

ABOVE: Metallica frontman, James Hetfield and Bruce Mayer, founding Chairman of the Petersen Automotive Museum get to work cutting the ribbon to officially open the exhibition.

LEFT: Relaxing after the opening is left to right: Bruce Mayer, James Hetfield, Rick Dore and Petersen Museum Executive Director Terry L. Karges.

OPPOSITE PAGE: These photos show some of the 10 cars in the exhibition as displayed on their own separate floodlit plinths for the period of the exhibition. A giant photo graces the wall in the background, showing Hetfield "at work" during a concert, providing the perfect backdrop to the cars in the exhibition.

FAR LEFT: James Hetfield shares a moment with the winner of the Snow White Snake Byte ESP guitar, one of two guitars that were auctioned at the opening.

Grease Pit", he was showing off the Buick to Dore. It was a green Skylark, bone stock driver. Hetfield then asked Dore, "Are you going to help me or not?" and that began a decades-long collaboration of the two craftsmen. Together they have built eleven customs.

Dore stated he loves all the customs he has worked on. He loves the smell of the leather and the memories these cars rekindle from the old times. He emphasized that all of the cars he built with Hetfield were "all drivers. The last few cars were great drivers with lots of miles on them." Hetfield notes that "a lot of the cars were an idea before we found a car."

Dore admits while growing up in Yonkers, New York he didn't get a chance to drive many cars but always had hot rod magazines in his room. After the Vietnam War, he had moved to Phoenix, Arizona and saw a chopped Mercury driving down the road. He pulled up to the Mercury and followed the owner home to learn more about the custom. From there he was hooked.

Dore bought a 1956 Buick and started his customizing path. In 1997, after building his "Tangerine Dream", a custom 1936 Ford, he realized he could make a business out of his work, with others approaching him to produce customs.

Dore admits to "not being a body man" and calls himself a "stylist". He modestly states he "knows what works and what doesn't" and "I have a good eye." Dore has always relied on others on his team to help produce his vision. Dore noted that with the cars at Reclaimed Rust, "these cars are true art. Hang them on the wall." He noted that, "Hetfield wanted the next generation to see them and be inspired to build their own cars. A car is an extension of a person."

Dore now lives in Nevada and enjoys going out to car shows and "I let people know I love their cars" when he sees one that catches the customizer's "eye". He added that "I was lucky and fortunate to get to the level of my peers" and "want people to like my cars. Hopefully in fifty years, people will be restoring these cars."

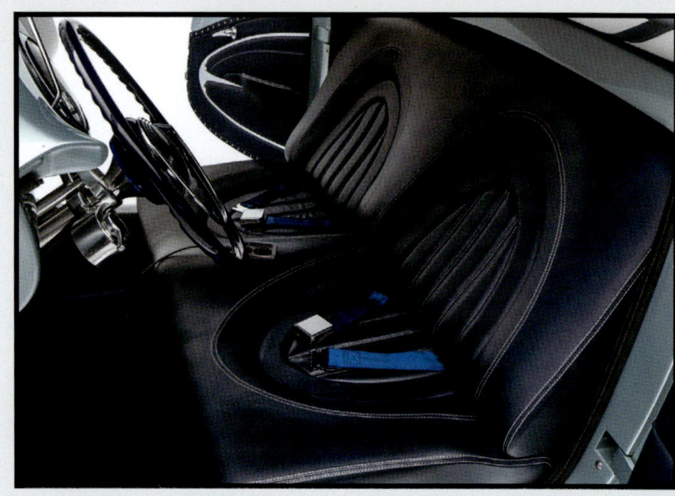

Aquarius

A collaboration between Hetfield, De Lay, and Dore this car borrowed some styling cues from a 1939 Delahaye and featured a removable hardtop. It rests on a 1934 Packard frame with a Chevy 6.2 liter LS3 engine under the hood. Hetfield wanted this car on a revolving pedestal so viewers could appreciate the car from all angles. Dore said, "I wanted to build one with the grace of French builds but with an American attitude".

Dore mentioned that in the past when asked which car his favorite was, his normal response was "the one I am working on now." But after finishing the Aquarius he has modified his answer, acknowledging that the Aquarius is his favorite, and rightfully so.

Black Jack

Hetfield kept the look of this 1932 Ford roadster but used parts that were period correct to make it a throwback hot rod. Ironically the car is not actually black. The grille, body, and hood are a dark, deep brown

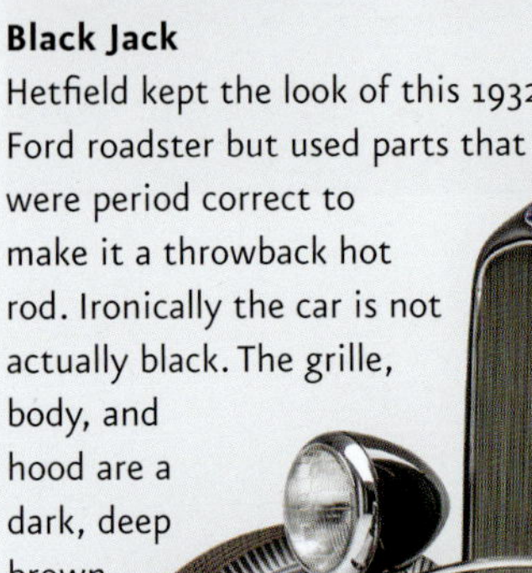

that looks nearly black. The Ford has a 296 CID (4.8 liter) Ford V8 under the hood. This was built by Josh Mills.

Str8 Edge

Hetfield took a 1956 Ford F100 truck with a stretched cab, added some angular quad headlights from a 1960 Ford, gave it a chop and a big rear window. The truck has a Mustang II front end and airbags create the stance.

The white pinstriping accented the lines of the purple hue truck. It runs with an Olds 455 CID (7.4 liter) engine. The truck bed and tailgate are based on a 1957 Ford Ranchero. This truck was built by Scott Mugford.

Black Pearl

Starting with a 1948 Jaguar sedan chassis, the bodywork was hand done by Marcel De Lay out of aluminum panels. Hetfield actually drew the basis for the shape of the car. The top featured a "chopped" look and the stance comes via airbags. There is a Ford 302 (4.9 liter) under the hood linked to a Ford C4 automatic. The deep black paint is emphasized with brass side trim.

Crimson Ghost

Hetfield has some strong attraction to Fords, this one is based on a 1937 coupe. The car was lowered, chopped, decked, shaved, and nosed. Dore also removed the "B pillar" on this Ford and added running boards. The rear fenders included fender skirts to hide the tires. Dore included a skull shifter knob in the two-seater interior. This was one of the earlier Dore-Hetfield collaborations.

Skyscraper

This car started the teamwork between Dore and Hetfield. Rick Dore took Hetfield's 1953 Buick Skylark and added those iconic custom touches, including a light purple pearl paint by Art Himsl. The front bumper was smoothed. The Buick was originally a convertible until Dore changed it into a hardtop. They placed a Chevy 350 (5.7 liter) V8 under the hood with an automatic transmission. In acknowledgment of Hetfield's musical roots, the gas pedal is shaped like a bass drum pedal and the dash gauges resemble guitar picks.

Iron Fist

This 1936 Ford five-window coupe showcases a basic hot rod look with the blue oval body stripped to bare metal and then covered in clear. It also rides on airbags and has a Mustang II front-end suspension. The hood was converted to a one-piece design. This Ford was also a Mugford build.

Voodoo Priest

Dore took a 1937 Lincoln Zephyr V-12 and modernized the full look of this build. The bodywork was heavily massaged with a lowered deck lid, new rear quarter panels, and redesigned doors. The V-12 4.4-liter engine uses three Stromberg carburetors and matches up to a C4 automatic transmission.

Dead Kennedy

A 1963 Lincoln Continental was customized with Hetfield doing all of the work on this car.

The paint was a flat black with a flaked black top. He kept the 430 CID (7 liter) V8 Lincoln motor.

Slowburn

Based on a 1936 Auburn, but in fiberglass, with a wild custom touch and another removable Carson-style hardtop. Dore kept the boat-tail rear end, sectioned the body, and added some pontoon fenders with skirts, to mix with a two-tone paint job. It is powered by a ZZ4 350 (5.7 liter) Chevy engine with a TH350 transmission. It rides on a set of wide whites to complete the look.

The car featured suicide doors and a custom ultra-wide grille and looks similar outwardly to the limousine ridden by President John F Kennedy in Dallas, Texas before his assassination. Hence the name of the car.

Rattletrap IV
DRAG-ENS HOT ROD CLUB

Words and Photos by: Al O'Toole

The Drag-Ens Hot Rod Club's Rattletrap IV took place at Crowdy Head on the NSW mid-north coast on Saturday May 8, 2021 and it was again a huge success with hundreds of people lining the beach to get a taste of ol' timey beach trials.

The Rattletrap has become a bucket list event for many people since launching in 2017 and has spawned a new breed of hot rod that enthusiasts are building specifically for fun on the sand. Of the 80 or so entrants that took part, over a dozen made the long journey to Crowdy Head from Victoria with many others travelling down from Queensland. Entries are taken via application with the event open to vintage hot rods, race cars and bikes. Cars must be manufactured on or before 1941, while bikes built prior to 1960 are eligible and should be hopped up like authentic vehicles from the pre to post war eras.

Rattletrap IV kicked off on the Friday afternoon with scrutineering held at the Harrington Beach Holiday and Caravan Park, while rodders took the opportunity to cruise the grounds in vehicles that seldom get used. This warm-up to the beach trials is a highlight for many and a great chance to catch up with friends

This is not a speed event and it's not racing, it's beach trials, and there are no prizes for crossing the finish line first. The Drag-Ens do award a Best Dressed award as participants, officials and spectators are encouraged to dress in period clothing to further enhance the old school atmosphere of Rattletrap.

This year the beach had lost quite a bit of sand due to large swells and the staging area was considerable smaller than at previous Rattletrap events. As a result the start line was moved further up the beach, but it didn't make much difference to the experience, everyone was smiling and having a great time.

After the trials were called off with the rising of the tide, hot rodders headed back to Harrington where everyone enjoyed wood-fired pizzas, or a feed at the pub or bowlo, live music and auctions that raised money for charity. Well done to the Drag-Ens on another awesome event, can't wait for next year! ∎

MAIN: Hayden Prendergast leads the way back to the start in his chopped and channelled '30 Model A Ford coupe.
RIGHT: Another patina flavoured Model A, this time it's Shaun Canavan's hiboy style coupe with flathead running gear and '35 Ford wire wheels.

ABOVE: Very basic T Model Ford based speedster is the perfect fun ride for Kelvin Wrigg to go racing at Rattletrap.

ABOVE: This hiboy Deuce roadster belongs to Paul Mortimer of the Barons Moto club and runs a 350 Chevy engine, Brookville reproduction steel body and '40s era Ford steel wheels.

ABOVE: Poppy's Jalopy from "Sweet & Silky Motors" is the Aussie bodied and flathead powered '34 Ford hiboy coupe that was entered by Corrine Black.

Rattletrap

LEFT: Paul McMullin's tri-powered flathead equipped Deuce roadster was built for having fun at events like Rattletrap. It's fun!

ABOVE: Screw it on and blast the beach.

ABOVE: Vultures club member, Wayne O'Grady hauled his Ardun equipped '33 Ford three window coupe up from Melbourne. Here he's taking on David Hunt in his Y block motivated speedway '37 Ford coupe.

RIGHT: Banger power is all Matt Ward needs to have fun at Rattletrap in his Model A roadster pickup.

ABOVE: Motorcycles up to 1960 are welcome at Rattletrap and this photo attests to how well they fit in. On the Indian is Craig Fischer hoping to catch up.

ABOVE: Alan Lock/Geoff Eldridge from Gumma, NSW entered the 1949 BSA C11 250, seen here running against Bruce Scott on his '38 Harley Davidson.
ABOVE RIGHT: Battle of the bellytanks with Gavan Starr-Thomas on the left and Warren Kranske on the right.
RIGHT: Patina covered El Camino is a '59 model that has been treated to a hefty lowering job and sports a rare venetion in the rear window.

RIGHT: Zacariah Ralph is neck and neck with Dave Pothecary while John Martin brings up the rear.
BELOW RIGHT: Amongst the spectator cars was Luke Pohl's gold big block Ford powered pickup next to Rhonda Longfield's red '32 Ford coupe.

ABOVE: Garry Winship in the 1940 Ford Fordor sedan makes his way back to the start line.

ABOVE: Andrew McClelland and Norm Hardinge take a pleasant drive along the beach on the way back to the start line.

ABOVE: Garry Ward's channelled T Coupe uses triple carbed Y block Ford engine to chase down John Rodriques in his twin carb flathead powered speedster.

ABOVE: In the car park was this tidy '36 Ford Tudor finished in grey and hunkered down over the steel wheels with caps and trim rings. Nice!

BELOW: Low profile 1930 Model A Ford coupe belongs to Hayden Prendergast from Brown Hill, Victoria. Six carbies on a 350 small block Chevy make it go, Firestone whitewalls make it look perfect for the era!

ABOVE: Pit talk – we were fast in the old days, but now we've got this Frenzel supercharger to make the old flathead really fly!

ABOVE RIGHT: Alex McDowell in the T bucket gets out in front of Garry Ward's channelled T coupe.

RIGHT: Here's a front on view of John Rodriques silver speedster. Dig the yellow spot lights in front of the familiar T grille surround.

MAIN: A line of competitors make their way back to the start line in front of a large crowd of spectators comfortably ensconced on the edge of the beach. That's James Brennan from Ipswich, Queensland in his centrifugally supercharged 4 BANGA Model A roadster at the tail of the line.

Rattletrap

RIGHT: Flathead powered '30 Model A Ford roadster of Chad Williams takes on Craig Lockhart in his red oxide '36 Ford three window coupe.

BELOW: "The Mongrel"T speedster, driven by Rod Hadfield leads this group of competitors back to the start line to prepare for another round of entertaining "racing".

LEFT: Raymond Colwell jumps to an early lead in his nicely finished 239 cubic inch flathead powered speedster that uses a '38 Ford chassis and hand-formed body. In the other lane is Rob Corben from the Thirlmere Idlewild Hot Rod Club in his black '32 flathead V8-powered Miller speedster replica special that uses '35 Ford wire wheels.

ABOVE: Rear view of Rod Hadfield's "Mongrel" T speedster that was originally built by Harold Ely of Castlemaine.

ABOVE: Warren Kranske returning to the staging area in the flathead V8 powered bellytank lakester, here it is on display with the body off after the trials finished.

RIGHT: John Rodriques flathead powered speedster is all you need to have fun at Rattletrap, it's not a race, it's a speed trial.

BELOW: Baron's Moto Club member Tim Miller in the AV8 roadster versus fellow member Roem Crompton in the '34 coupe. The roadster sports a twin carb fed flathead equipped with a reproduction Frenzel Supercharger.

BELOW RIGHT: Winners of Best Dressed were Bronwyn Sainty and her partner.

Rattletrap

ABOVE: Kevin Boardman from Narrawa, NSW in the yellow 1915 Model T takes on Andrew Paronis from Bankstown, NSW in his '28 Model A Ford Pickup.

ABOVE LEFT: Gavan Starr-Thomas looks set to take on the world in his bellytank "Beachster".

LEFT: Benjamin Watson from Marrickville, NSW 1942 Harley Davidson WLA on the left, Ben Cooley on the right.

BELOW: Hiboy Model a roadster of James Brennan versus the severely chopped Model A coupe entered by Damien Kemp.

BELOW: Craig Lockhart from Wonglepong in Queensland pedals his 1936 Ford three window coupe against the 1930 Model A Ford coupe of Hayden Prendergast from Brown Hill, Victoria.

ABOVE & ABOVE LEFT: Getting back off the beach up the soft, sandy exit track at the end of the day's play was part of the adventure for the drivers.

LEFT: Chris Gill built this little flathead powered T bucket for the event but only got one run down the sand thanks to a wayward clutch fork. That's Ben Watson's small block Ford powered '28 Model A roadster pickup next to the motorbike in the near background. Further over in the background, the trailers are loaded ready for the trip home.

ABOVE: The Jaunty Jalopy banger powered Model A of Steve Fleming takes on the T bucket based beachster of Alex McDowell is also banger powered, but fitted with twin carbs.

THIS PAGE Top to Bottom: More photos of competitors bouncing up the sandy track to exit the beach at the end of the day's racing. Rod Hadfield had a ball at Rattletrap, seen here exiting the beach with Norm Hardinge riding shotgun in/on "The Mongrel" Model T race-about special that gets a helping hand from a pushing party. Mick Petith struck a problem while trying to ride his 1941 Indian Scout up the soft, sandy exit track. The crowd stayed around to watch the antics until the very end.

ABOVE: Channelled two door '32 Ford tourer looks like a fun ride for John McClelland. Note the megaphone exhaust hooked up to the stock manifold – it's all about having fun with what you've got!

ABOVE LEFT: Thumbs up and smiles all 'round at Rattletrap IV. George Livas entered his 221 flathead powered '26 Ford roadster, but he's been bumped from behind the wheel for this trip back up the return road.

MAIN: Number 69 is Kenton McKay from Ningi, Queensland in his flathead V8 powered '27 T Ford roadster. Running in the next lane is Roem Crompton in his '34 Ford five window coupe from Palmswood, Queensland.

BELOW: The Model A hiboy roadster of James Brennan has centrifugal blower on the banger engine. Damien Kemp owns the chopped 1930 Model A coupe that runs a 327 Chevy dressed as an Olds Rocket V8.

MEGA DEUCE

IS MEGA BAD

THE B&M/BRIZIO "MEGA DEUCE"

1932 FORD TUDOR

By Greg Stokes

MEGA DEUCE

Back in 2012 I had the good fortune to be loaned Andy Brizio's "Rodfather" '32 Ford roadster for Hot Rod Week leading up to the Goodguys, West Coast Nationals in Pleasanton, California. Incredibly lucky to be driving the famous purple flamed roadster, I also had a first-hand impression as to how good a Brizio-built hot rod actually looks. From that moment on it was a dream to one day own a professional Brizio-built hot rod. Fast forward to 2020 when the car you see here came up for sale. Wow, the original B&M/Brizio 1932 Ford Tudor "Mega Deuce" from Rod & Custom Magazine circa 1995 was now available!

While I wasn't in a position to act, I knew just the man who could. Good friends don't let good friends drive bad cars right? Enter very good friend, Ian Taylor, a founding member of the Early Ford V8 Club of NZ and a member of the Pukekohe Hot Rod Club. After a lifetime of early Ford V8s, he surprised all when he ordered a brand new 2018 Dodge Demon. At this stage of his life it was well past a mid-life crisis and then the following year he bought a big block Chev powered 1932 Ford coupe. I must add, that it's the gentleman-like nature of the man, that Ian is very humble of his diverse car collection which he describes as "just a couple of cars" with a cheeky grin.

His collection is an incredible mix of lovely restored early Ford V8's and beautifully immaculate hot rods – he loves it all and loves the people he meets. Ian, like many in the automotive hobby of his age, now starts looking at things as to how many summers are left. This mindset is a stark comparison to the time in the early '90s when he sat in Ian Goodwin's upholstery shop, while the interior was being done on John Reid's "BILIT" Model A coupe – "I am gonna own that car one day," he said. Ian Taylor has been a great loyal friend to me and we'd hang out often. Jokingly over lunch one weekend I said, "what are you going to buy this year mate?" His reply was, "My wife would kill me if I got another car!" But we talked and it was Ian's closing comment, which he would look at the "right" thing if it came along.

Then one day online at Opposingcylinders.com, a particular car turned up for sale that tugged all the heart strings of my hot rodding interests and I called Ian. "You won't believe what's for sale at killer money, a Brizio built B&M project 1932 Ford hiboy Tudor with Halibrands and a quick change and a blown big block". His dry reply wa, "Heck I already have one big block – let me think about it." An hour later he calls back, "Greg, a car like that isn't really me to be honest, I am more about fenders and bumpers and so on but what do you think?" Well, I didn't need to harp on about what I thought as that was a given. A couple of weeks later the price was reduced and I called Ian again, we talked some more and he said if it goes a bit lower that he would look at it.

A couple of weeks passed and the price was at what Ian said he would look at, so I call him back and say it's at your dollar. "Yeah but what's wrong with it?" he laughs. Hmmm, I had thought that too. "If it weren't for COVID restrictions, we could jump on a plane and check it out," jokes Ian. A couple of weeks later another price reduction that led to Ian's request for me to call up and see what they would take. I'm thinking heck you couldn't buy the engine for what they are asking, so I call Sid Chavers selling it on behalf of the owner, Scott Hawley. "Hey Sid, how's things? What's the go with the price reductions? Does it ride good? Does it overheat?". All answered positively as you would expect, it is a Brizio-built car and Scott just wants to thin the herd. "Yeah I should probably do that myself!" laughs Ian as I relay it all back to him and then he says, "Yep, let's do it, what do you think?"

Of course I am more than happy to see this deal go down, like how many chances in life does one get to be this close to an iconic car? We talk some more and Ian refers back to that stage of his life where he wants to enjoy every moment of what's left and he wants to share the fun. How awesome is that? We all talk of living the ultimate life (which differs for each and every one of us) and here is a guy who has worked hard in the same job his whole life and now in his early seventies (still working) and wants to enjoy the benefit of his work and careful planning.

MEGA DEUCE

www.graffitipub.com.au

The car was shipped out of Oakland, California late January 2021 and 42 days later travelling via Alaska, Seattle and then back down to Long Beach. The car arrived in Auckland, and what a Friday that was to watch the container open to reveal a damage free perfect 1932 Tudor that seriously screamed HOT ROD!. Previous owner Scott, and Sid and also Roy Brizio were naturally brilliant to deal with and it was a pleasure to call Scott and say, "Thanks man – it's here and its safe and sound!" Scott was genuinely excited for us, "Have you started it up, it should run and smell sweet on 110 octane gas." Sure to his word, the starter cranked over and the B&M supercharged, Bill Mitchell built 510 cubic inch big block Chev fired into life with a super responsive throttle and a very happy idle. Could this day have got any better?

Back home at GMS Hot Rods, we just stood in awe. A well-known Brizio-built 1932 Ford hot rod was sitting there right in front of us – very surreal. A wee drive up the road gave an idea as to how smooth the car drives despite 850hp under your right foot. Back home it was time to check the car out and start repolishing a lot of dulled off alloy and stainless. It's not until you get this up close and personal to a car that you realise and discover all the cool details and build techniques. It was a true case of the more you looked, the better it became. The car came with a very comprehensive folder with every invoice, time sheet and any dialogue pertaining to the car inside – very interesting reading!

Roy Brizio remembers "Mega Deuce was one of my most favourite builds, inspired by the Phil Kendrick '32 Tudor of the '60s, Thom Taylor did the initial renderings and then we got to work." The build started in January 1995 and then made the cover of the March 1996 Rod & Custom Magazine finished. Frank Ghiglione, commissioned the build with Roy Brizio Street Rods and B&M Racing with Rod & Custom Magazine publishing the build of the B&M/Brizio Project Car with other suppliers stepping up to be involved. This car was the last of six B&M based street rods to be built. Cast your mind back to Roy Brizio's personal scalloped B&M project '32 roadster, B&M's very own Jim Davis had a red full fendered B&M project '32 roadster, the late Pete Chapouris built the Limefire B&M project '32 roadster, Boyce Asquith built the street/strip B&M project '32 roadster, John Mumford has the Brizio built B&M project '32 three window coupe and then there is the B&M project '32 Tudor you see here – Mega Deuce. Frank was a trucking company owner with a 50 plus vehicle car collection and once the car was completed it didn't really get out much other than a few events including Roy taking the car to Andy's Picnic in 1996. Up until seven years ago the car had only 936 miles on it when another Brizio customer, Scott Hawley stepped up and purchased the rarely seen, but iconic car. He sent the car back to Roy's for a freshen up of sorts with fluids changed, parts and wheels repolished, new tyres fitted all round before bringing the mileage up to just a tad over 2000 miles. Hawley also displayed the car at GNRS in 2017 on the Roy Brizio Street Rods booth.

This brings us to the present day and the sequence of events that resulted in Ian Taylor owning the car after I pestered Ian for nearly a month to buy such a thing. We laughed to each other like school kids as the car was on the water and mutual friends of ours would say, "That's not the type of car for Ian but it sure is all what Greg likes!" Interestingly, a lot of people recall seeing the car at its brief appearances or remember reading about it in Rod & Custom Magazine. Some USA based rodders were shocked to hear it had left their country to spend the rest of its life in the Land of the Long White Cloud. Either way, for good reason, this car has made an impact on a lot of people. One of them is Jack Stratton, head fabricator at Brizios who remembers building the car, "Such a bitchin' car and it was a lot of fun to build," he said. Both Ian and I are just really enjoying getting to know the car. The LVVTA certification process was completed thanks to Mark Stokes of M.S. Vehicle Certification and we are looking forward to attending many events with the car. Like all of his cars, Ian Taylor is the right guy to own something like this as he sure knows how to keep all his cars in top condition from top to bottom. For me personally I cannot thank Ian enough entrusting me with the car and giving me the golden opportunity to treat the car as if it were my own. The New Zealand hot rodding scene is further enriched with the arrival of this high quality professional USA built hot rod. ◼

MEGA DEUCE

SPECIFICATIONS: Ian Taylor – Pukekohe Hot Rod Club – 1932 Ford Tudor

Maintenance, certification work and post shipping clean up and detail by Greg Stokes, GMS Hot Rods.

BODY

Original Henry Ford 1932 Ford Tudor
Chopped 2 ½" with a filled roof and cowl vent by Marcel Delay.
Bitchin Products recessed firewall
Peaked 1932 Ford radiator surround with polished stainless Dan Fink grille insert
Three piece alloy hood by Jack Hagemann
Dan Fink 3 pce hood hinge and latch kit
Rear rolled pan by Jack Hagemann
King Bee headlights
1941 Ford taillights

CHASSIS

Just-a-Hobby rails with custom tubular centre section, front crossmember pushed forward – all chassis fabrication by Jack Stratton at Brizio's.
Mullins Vega steering box
Stainless brake lines throughout

FRONT SUSPENSION

Superbell 5" dropped axle
Superbell polished Wilwood brakes
Brizio fabricated hairpins
Durant spring
Pete & Jakes chrome shocks

REAR SUSPENSION

Halibrand Champ rear end (4.11 ring gear with a 3.5 final gear)
Pete & Jakes ladder bars
Deuce Factory rear sway bar
Aldan coil-overs
Wilwood brakes

WHEELS & TYRES

Halibrand "Sweet Swirl" directional wheels with full Halibrand directional knock-off kit
F 15x5 ½ & R 15x11
Hoosier Pro Street Radial tyres
F 26x7.50x15 & R 31x16.50x15

SPECIFICATIONS: Ian Taylor – Pukekohe Hot Rod Club – 1932 Ford Tudor

ENGINE

Big block Chev 510 cu. in. by Bill Mitchell Hardcore Racing Products
World Products Merlin Heads
B&M Mega Blower 420
Twin 750 Holley chromed carbs
BDS polished dual scoop
Holley fuel system
Mezerie electric water pump
Mallory/MSD ignition
Stainless Limefire style headers by Jack Stratton at Brizio's leading
into a full stainless system with Megs tips

TRANSMISSION

B&M Racing TH400 gearbox (polished case option)
B&M SFI flexplate
B&M 2500 stall Holeshot converter
B&M Street Rod trans cooler

PAINT

Dupont Hemi Orange by the Toy Works
Tommy the Greek style striping by Rory

INTERIOR

Black leather with black wool headliner and carpets by Howdy
Ledbetter
Teas Design adjustable bucket seats
Specialty power window kit
Custom covers over rear gas tank
Chrome four point roll bar
Moon gauges
Pete & Jakes steering wheel and column
B&M Pro Stick shifter
Lokar handbrake
Spoon throttle pedal

OTHER

Wiring by Jim Vickery at Brizio's
All plumbing by Earl's Fittings
Chrome plating & polishing by Sherm's Custom Plating
Griffen split core smooth top radiatior
Moon 3-1/2 gal tank
Featured in March 1996 Rod & Custom Magazine (on cover), Roy Brizio
Street Rods book by Bo Bertilson, The Original Hot Rod – DEUCE book
by Mike Chase. Goodguys 2020 Hot Rod of the Year Finalist.

After taking a year off, the Specialty Equipment Market Association (SEMA) held its annual trade show in Las Vegas, Nevada in November 2021. The SEMA Show had been cancelled for 2020, but for 2021 they came back strong and even used the newly constructed West Hall for the show.

Over 1300 exhibitors had displays at the Las Vegas Convention Center and one easy way to get the attention of passers-by is to have at least one display vehicle at your booth. A little eye candy is a great way to draw in a crowd and rods and customs are a definite draw to the show. With 230,000 square metres of interior space, there was plenty of space to house a few cars and trucks.

ABOVE: Ford unveiled a 1969 Ford Mustang that was restored for country singer Keith Urban. A gift from his wife and actress, Nicole Kidman, for their second wedding anniversary, it languished in a shop until Ford and the SEMA Garage heard of the predicament, so common to many classic car owners, and rescued it. The dark blue Mustang was fully customized and returned to Urban. They squeezed in a Ford V8 linked to a Rousch supercharger with a ten-speed automatic transmission.

ABOVE & LEFT: "Born 49ain" was inspired by the post-apocolyptic world of Mad Max. The '49 Ford shoebox has been chopped four inches, shortened seven inches and body-dropped over a BMW 335i complete with all of its running gear and creature comforts. It rolls on monstrous 20x12 and 20x14 inch Hostile truck wheels and was built on a budget by John Malazsak after a 15 year hiatus from custom car building, just to show what a few friends working together can achieve and to inspire others to follow their dreams.

ABOVE: Chevrolet revived the 1957 Project X Chevy, featured by Popular Hot Rodding magazine since 1965 as they showed off a variety of alterations over the years. Look closely and you'll see no exhaust pipes sticking out from the rear. That's because the crew at Chevrolet installed an electric drive unit that is a plug and play crate "engine".

ABOVE: Sinners Rat Rod - Built not bought '30 Model A Tudor fitted with a 5.9lt Cummins turbo diesel and half-track.

BELOW: Gateway Bronco offered up their LUXE-GT electrified 1972 Bronco. The batteries allow a 480 kilometer range and 0-100 kph in less than five seconds via a Legacy EV 540 volt drive train. It rides on 84 cm Toyo tires and an electric ride control suspension from JRi Shocks.

BELOW: This 1969 Camaro featured Blacktech's Forged Carbon hood, featuring a large-tow woven carbon in a chopped and marbled application backed with traditional woven fabric for an eye catching look. The hood features functional air ducts. It also had carbon fiber side mirrors, trunk lid and rear spoiler.

ABOVE & RIGHT: John Oro's 1971 Chevy K5 Blazer "Prom Queen" had suspension surgery done by Metalox Fab, with a Porterbuilt chassis and Air Lift suspension. It rides on American Racing wheels and utilized some LED lights for a modern touch. Powered by an LS crate engine it carries Oro, President of Arizona's C10 Club, easily down the boulevards.

Plus more outdoor space is allocated for vehicles. That is how thousands of cars end up at the SEMA Show. You see everything from stock vehicles to wild custom creations. Sometimes words can't express how wild and outrageous these rides are.

Not only do the major auto manufacturers have their own display space but plenty of vendors will use new and old vehicles to show off their latest wares and products. In addition, the exterior space of the convention center is filled up with sponsored cars that did not gain a coveted spot inside.

It was not a surprise to see a string of Ford Broncos at the SEMA show this year. No wonder they are hard to find at a dealership, they were all at SEMA. Perhaps the most breathtaking Bronco was a one-off custom red Bronco pickup truck. The crew at BDS Suspension took a Bronco Diamond Elite model, chopped off the back and created a pickup designated as a Fire Command truck. They repurposed some Ford Ranger parts for the tailgate. The folks at Ford were so impressed they ended up giving it one of their coveted design awards.

Also at the Ford display, Jay Leno led their press conference where they unveiled a 1969 Ford Mustang that was restored for country singer Keith Urban. It seems that his wife and actress, Nicole Kidman, had bought it in 2008 to celebrate their second wedding anniversary. They took it to a shop to be restored and it languished there indefinitely. Eventually, Ford and the SEMA Garage heard of the predicament, so common to many classic car owners, and rescued it. The leads from Ford and the SEMA Garage said the car was in bad shape, despite the past restoration efforts. The driver's door nearly came off the hinges when being inspected and the front bumper was being secured using Vise-grips.

Well after some long hours, the dark blue Mustang was fully customized and returned to Urban. They squeezed in a Ford V8 linked to a Rousch supercharger with a ten-speed automatic transmission. The Mustang should put out 700 horsepower. The car came with Forgeline wheels, Bilstein shocks, and Wilwood brakes. Fender Guitar even crafted a new guitar with a similar paint scheme to go with the car. It was interesting to see that even "stars" can have issues with their cars and it was nice to see it finally resolved so successfully.

Gateway Bronco showed off their 1972 F-350 "Godzilla" truck. The company is now licensed from Ford to offer more classic Ford

LEFT: "Many window" Kombi splitty van with sliding sun-roof looks amazing in striking two tone finish.

BELOW: Dave Kindig brought out his unique design, a "CF1 roadster" with a carbon fiber body matched to a Lingenfelter LS7 engine with a Borla stacked injection unit. It certainly has some lines and hints from a 1953 Corvette but it is wider and longer than an original C1 Corvette.

BELOW LEFT: Truck of the Year is a 1955 Chevrolet Cameo built by Mike Goldman Customs and powered by an LS7 engine.

BELOW: Chip Foose brought out several of his builds to this year's show, including the "Impostor" a 1965 Impala Sport Coupe resting on a new 2009 Corvette chassis. To make it fit the chassis was stretched 20cm while the Impala's body was shortened 35cm. The Impala won the 2015 Ridler Award at the Detroit, MI Autorama.

TOP LEFT: 1966 Impala "Ice Breaker" owned by Samson Fernandez has an awesome paint job by Bugs Auto Art from Mesa, AZ along with a solid sound system from Fish Designz. It was sponsored by Anest Iawa.

LEFT: Chip Foose's 1932 five window Ford was part of the huge Foose display. His personal build had a '40s style. It held a flathead V8 with a supercharger and a 1939 Ford toploader. The rear and front brakes are from a 1940 Lincoln. The custom billet Foose wheels have a Halibrand flair to them.

ABOVE: Dave Kindig had this 1951 Ford F-1 in the Borla booth. The owners had it since the 1980s. It had been transformed on his Bitchin' Rides TV Show. Kindig stretched the cabin and replaced the door handles with his own design. The pickup is painted a Bad Blood Red Pearl/Candy and that truck bed had a distinctive hourglass shape.

Trucks and is ramping up production. This one was powered by a 7.3-liter engine with a Harrop supercharger with an estimated 1,000+ horsepower. The truck has a six-speed automatic. The wood bed came from used barn wood for a different look.

Chip Foose took advantage of some excess floor space and brought out twenty of his builds for folks to gaze and drool over. Most of these cars are owned by the Petersen Museum, car enthusiasts, and collectors, so it was nice to see all agree to ship them over to Las Vegas for the four-day show. Four of the cars were past Ridler award winners and one of Foose's cars had won America's Most Beautiful Roadster (AMBR) award.

Of course, Chevrolet came out with a large display of both new cars and concept cars. This year they also revived the 1957 Project X Chevy. This car was featured by Popular Hot Rodding magazine since 1965 in numerous issues as they showed off a variety of alterations over the years. It also had a role in the 1980 movie, The Hollywood Knights. But this latest alteration from Chevrolet may be the biggest and badest yet. Look closely and you'll see no exhaust pipes sticking out from the rear. That's because the crew at Chevrolet installed an electric drive unit that is a proposed plug and play crate "engine". They estimate the unit will produce 340 horsepower and 440 Nm of torque. They were using a lithium-ion battery with 400 volts and 30kWh of energy, stored in the trunk. They also slipped in a quick change rear end for the chance to change out the overall ratio.

Dave Kindig brought out his unique design, a "CFI roadster" with a carbon fiber body matched to a Lingenfelter LS7 engine with a Borla stacked injection unit. The car is rated at 673 horsepower and 837 Nm of torque. It certainly has some lines and hints from a 1953 Corvette, but with the Kindig-it Design special touches. It is wider and longer than an original C1 Corvette.

A custom blue 1955 Chevrolet Bel Air built by Robert Matranga won the eighth annual Battle of the Builder competition. Over 240 vehicles were entered into the competition in four categories; Young Guns, Truck and Off-Road, Sport Compact/Impact, and Hot Rod. The field is narrowed to the Top 40 and then the Top 12. Those twelve finalists then judge each other's cars and vote for the best car.

The SEMA Show is held annually in Las Vegas, Nevada, and is the second-largest convention held in that town. This year over 50,000 registered buyers walked through over the four days of the event. Unfortunately, the SEMA Show is trade-only, so the general public cannot see these awesome builds in person. So enjoy the pictures we took of some of our favorite rides. ■

MAIN: Known as the Fast Layne 50, this 1950 Chevy pickup was built by L&S Customs in Prospect Hill, North Carolina, for Keith Layne of nearby Eden. Canyon Beige paint to cover those body panels as well as the dress-up components on the 425hp LS3 crate motor.

BELOW LEFT: "Coolair", the Chip Foose customized 1954 Chevy Bel Air includes a lowered roofline, frenched headlights with 1955 Chevy eyebrow trim, and similar frenched taillights. It sports a 1956 front bumper and the wheel wells were enlarged to show off those wheels. The engine was upgraded to a 2006 LS7 specification with LS6 heads and 7 liter displacement.

BELOW RIGHT: Jeremy Rice, owner of Tri-5 Customs built this 1950 Chevy 3100 in one year. Rice intends to use "Stifty" with a LS3 crate engine with a high output cam as his "shop truck". The inner and outer fenders were welded together for a smooth look to match the modified firewall. Rice frenched the headlights before adding LEDs.

RIGHT: In the Battle of the Builders competition, only one can be pronounced the overall winner. Robert Matranga's '55 Chevy took the award this year with his show-stopping Tri-Five, dubbed "Brute Force". Robert's Chevy won out over more than 240 other top show cars to win the competition.

BELOW: "FLO" started with a 1962 F-100 truck, but then the build fitted a 1964 raised bed with a custom tailgate stamped with "FLO" on a new custom chassis. They added a 2017 Mustang Gen 2 Coyote engine and a six-speed automatic transmission in this three month build, before originally showing up at the 2018 SEMA Show. Copper highlights make the black paint pop.

RIGHT: EV conversions were the hot topic at SEMA 2021 with plenty of examples on hand, but amongst the most interesting were the cast-aluminum cases for hiding motors and inverters in hot rods by Webb Motorworks. The one shown here was based on a mock-up of the Lincoln Zephyr V12, but they also make a small block Chevy version. Whether you dislike the "pretend" approach or not, the castings look sharp and they look better than a typical "undressed"EV motor.

LEFT: Joe Stupor owns this resto-mod 1959 Chevy Brookwood two-door wagon that sits flat on the pavement, sports superb two tone paintwork, and Tomahawk D concave wheels from Schott with low-profile tires. Mom's wagon certainly looks a bit different to the one she drove to the grocery store in 1959. Side trim is echos that from a 1956 Nomad. Under the hood is a detailed Chevy LS3.

RIGHT: Chip Foose designed "P32" as a tribute to rat rods and the post World War II era. He started with a '32 Ford and a Brookville body. He lowered it and added 5cm to the doors by shortening the front body panels. He kept a rat look by leaving untouched all the rivets and welds, using bomber seats from a B-17 plane while painting it olive drab. He put a flathead Lincoln V12 in the engine bay with the exhaust tips modeled after a P40 plane's exhaust

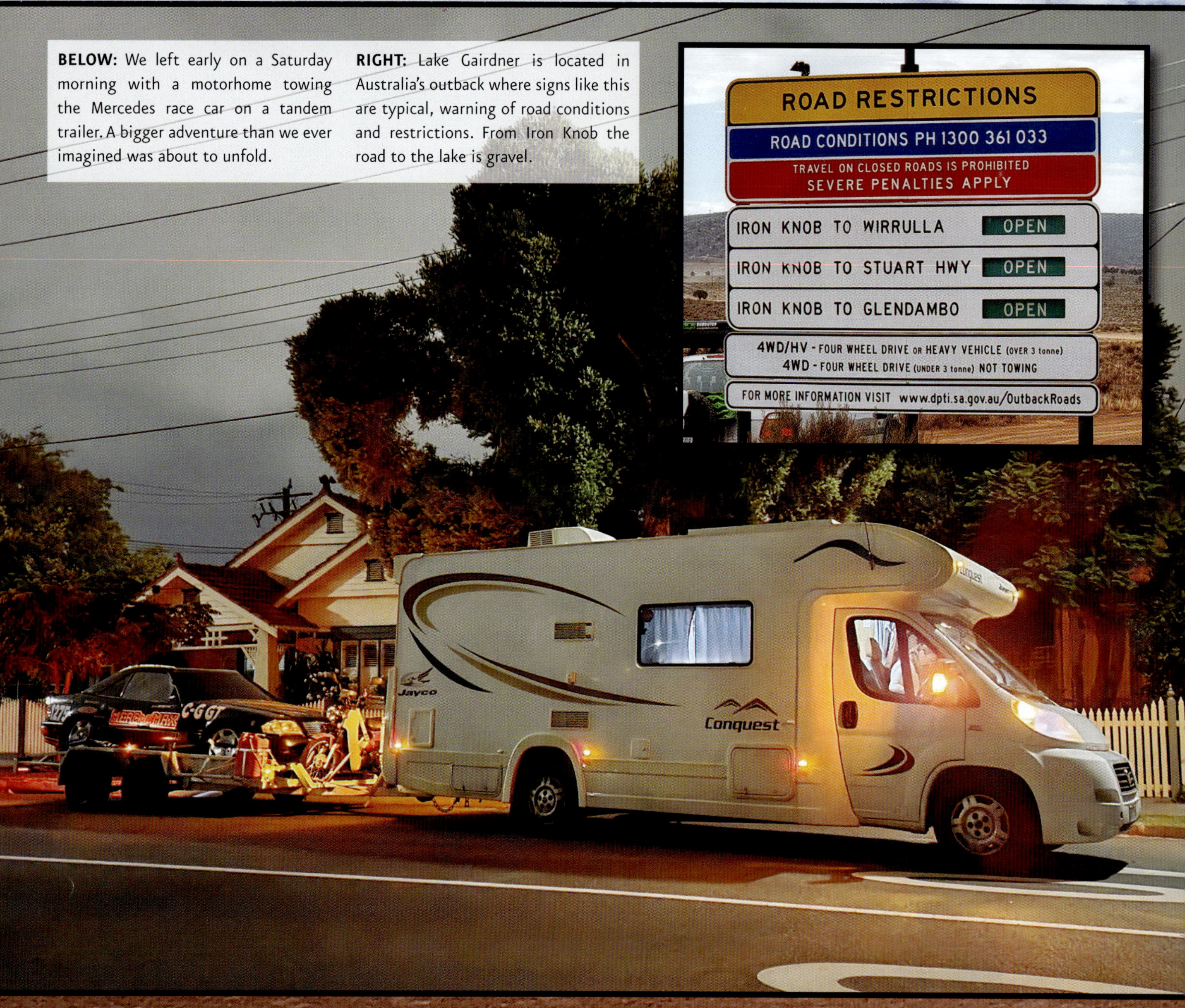

BELOW: We left early on a Saturday morning with a motorhome towing the Mercedes race car on a tandem trailer. A bigger adventure than we ever imagined was about to unfold.

RIGHT: Lake Gairdner is located in Australia's outback where signs like this are typical, warning of road conditions and restrictions. From Iron Knob the road to the lake is gravel.

I wanted to share the dreaded story of getting the salt lake racing car to Lake Gairdner and all the obstacles almost beyond belief. You could not make this stuff up.

I have been working on the car, trying to get it ready for the race for five or six years and the task just seemed to be getting bigger as we went along.

Then last year the race was cancelled – one week prior, due to COVID. So we thought it was ready for 2021, on the Wednesday before the weekend we were due to leave for the salt lake, we had the car down at the dyno workshop putting it through its paces. The gearbox started to fail, so on Thursday we removed and stripped it and Friday we repaired the gearbox and reinstalled it.

I was leaving on early Saturday morning with the motorhome to pull the car on a tandem trailer to the lake, so off we went in the dark. Hours later the water pump died and we could not go on. It was Saturday and there were no parts available as it

LEFT: When the water pump died on the motorhome we returned to Melbourne and headed off again in my street Mercedes family car – not your ideal tow vehicle for an adventure into the outback!

BELOW: Finally we were able to tow the race car out onto the salt lake and take up our spot in the pits where we could prepare for the tech inspection. Several safety related items were found and required rectification before we could be cleared to race, but at least we were finally at the salt lake.

was a long weekend, so we got the motorhome towed back to Melbourne, and then we came home and got the family car that has a tow bar. We hooked up the trailer and threw a few things in the boot, like underwear and toiletries, and away we went again. I was not going to miss out on the races, it was Saturday night by then, nothing was going to stop me getting there.

During the night we stopped at the township of Keith and slept for a few hours over the wheel. We were hoping to get to the salt lake by 4:00pm on Sunday as that is when they hold the drivers meeting. The road into the lake is dirt and bad in some places, it becomes very rocky going on to the edge of the salt lake and there were several long stretches with lots of bull dust that were very tricky, to say the least. But we made it to the salt lake, unfortunately too late for the drivers meeting.

The race car had moved forward on the trailer and it was putting a lot of weight on the car's tow bar that made the back of

the car almost scrape on the ground and it was kissing the bigger rocks as we went in.

There is a homestead 35 kilometres from the lake where we were able to book a room/shearers quarters to sleep in. We left the race car on the lake and headed back to the homestead. It had been a big few days, had dinner, a shower and a sleep. Wow we are here!

I woke at 3:00am and was thinking if I go back to Port Augusta in the morning and hire a four wheel drive we could sleep in it next to the salt lake, because I did not think going in and out would be very good for my city slicker car, so off we went to get a hire car, but there were none available in Port Augusta or even in Adelaide – they were scarce. We found a contact number on a hire car fence and they had one. They came in and we were set and soon on our way back to the salt lake. We had also purchased an air mattress, two pillows and two sleeping bags to sleep at the camp site next to the lake.

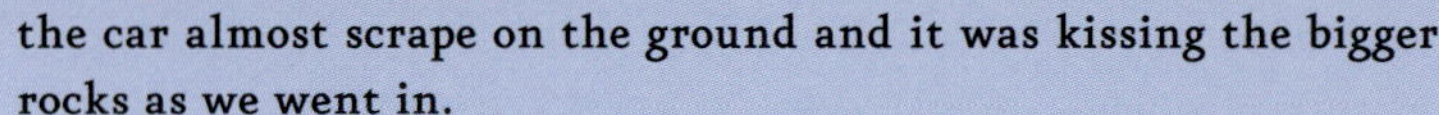

LEFT & BELOW: Not only is the car thoroughly checked over by the scrutineers, but so is the driver and all his related safety equipment. Several items, such as helmets, are dated and must be within date compliance to be able to be used. Finally, each driver has to perform a bail-out test. He is fully belted into the driver's seat, just as if ready to race and then has to be able to extricate himself from the vehicle within a set time. Racing is a dangerous sport, so no short cuts are taken when it comes to sfety. As a result dry lakes racing has a very good safety record.

That afternoon we presented the car to scrutineering and they found about 10 things that needed changing, mainly safety items. We worked all the next day and rectified most of the items, it was a big job, there were four of us including the help of Dean, a great effort was made by everybody. Then we went back to scrutineering and they passed us to race, so off to the starting line we went, and we were the last car for the day. I had been waiting for this moment for six years!

When we were going to the starting line, smoke started to fill the cabin. "Oh no," I thought, hoping it may be something simple... but the gearbox had died at the start line. The oil from the gearbox was pouring out and burning on the hot exhaust. Our race for 2021 was over.

That was that, we did not get to race, then back to the camp site and discussed regrets. In the morning it started to rain and rain, as we packed up to head home to Melbourne. The dirt road and the

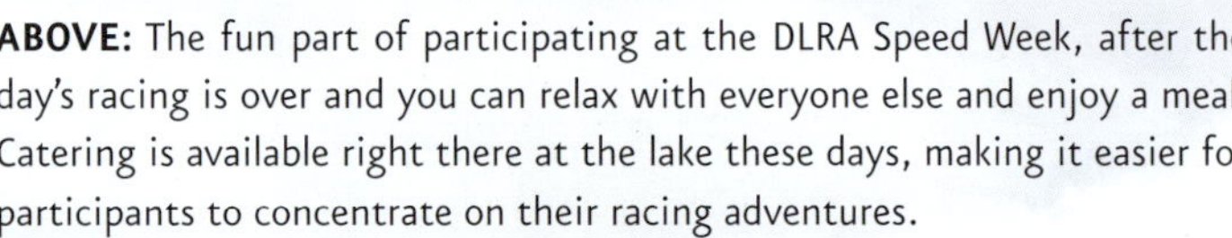

ABOVE: The fun part of participating at the DLRA Speed Week, after the day's racing is over and you can relax with everyone else and enjoy a meal. Catering is available right there at the lake these days, making it easier for participants to concentrate on their racing adventures.

ABOVE: Back home it was time to remove the transmisison again and find out what failed when we were on the start line and ready to go for our first run. The Mercedes will be back next year, better prepared and ready to take on the big white dyno.

bulldust holes turned very slippery and soon converted to mud and bog holes. The hired four wheel drive did a fantastic job getting us out, but we blew one of the trailer tyres on the way on the rough dirt road.

Then into Port Augusta to return the four wheel drive, book a room and have a nice meal and a sleep. The next day we set off for Melbourne again and had yet another tyre blow out on the trailer.

Home safe at last, lots to do before the salty next year, where do we start? Cleaning it up I suppose is a good place to begin and formulate a plan for next year. I will try to buy a semi-trailer for the race car in the next few months .

Wow what a trip, what an adventure, we will not forget Speed Week soon.

Normally bad luck comes in threes and when the gearbox died

ABOVE: Heavy rain made the trek out from Lake Gairdner another adventure in logistics. Add in a couple of trailer tyre blow-outs for good measure.
RIGHT: The trailer back on the street car for the final leg back to Melbourne.

in Melbourne before we left, I was a bit worried, but when the motorhome died, that was number two. I was starting to get quite concerned as bad things often come in threes. Will I have a big crash on the salt? Perhaps, but I cannot stop now.

When the gearbox died on the starting line that was number three, so we were right then. I would survive.

I woke up about 3:00am after the failure at the starting line and we were laying on an air mattress under the stars, I could not believe how content I was, there I was warm with my partner beside me and looking with amazement at the stars and the wonderful universe and feeling so, so lucky and content.

Yes, we will be there next year to try again – but better prepared.
Peter Max.

Stepping up to First Class
AMELIA ISLAND 2021
CONCOURS D'ELEGANCE

Words & Photos: Gerry Burger

From the Familiar to Obscure, Rarities and Racers, it was all there!

The Amelia Island Concours d'Elegance is the formal name, but to car guys it is simply "The Amelia". Twenty-six years ago, Bill Warner and a group of like-minded lovers of all things automotive thought scenic Amelia Island, Florida would be the perfect location for a great car show, and so it began. It is doubtful even Warner himself could have envisioned that first-year show blossoming into one of the finest automobile shows in the world. Today the comparisons to Pebble Beach are inevitable.

The "big show" itself has always been held on the second weekend in March. Due to a conflict the 2020 Concours was forced to move to the first weekend in March, a change that literally saved the show, as days later COVID hit, bringing automotive activities to a screeching halt. This year, because of COVID, the show was pushed to May, that turned out to be perfect timing as the outdoor mask mandate was lifted just a week prior to the show. And so, for many, (this author included) The Amelia was the last show attended in 2020 and the first show attended in 2021. After being cocooned in my garage for fourteen-months, I can think of no better way to re-enter the car hobby.

RIGHT: The 2022 version of The Amelia Island Concours d'Elegance will have a special class dedicated to ninety years of the 1932 Ford. These two hot rods are a sneak peek into next year's show, we can hardly wait.

ABOVE: Just imagine, it's 1938 and this streamlined, futuristic, Hispano-Suiza H6B Dubonnet Xenia glides by. It was said the Xenia delivers "the suppleness of a cat". Custom coachwork by Jacques Saoutchik, it was designed by Andre Dubonnet, an ace fighter pilot during WW-I turned designer. The car was hidden during WW-II and resurfaced in 1946, and there is much more to the story.

Like many great shows, the Concours de 'Elegance is simply the crown jewel ending to an automotive week that includes multiple car auctions, The Eight Flags Driving Tour to the scenic town of Fernandina Beach, seminars, a Porsche gathering call The Werks Reunion and the second biggest show of the week… Cars & Coffee at the Concours. This event is a simple nine till two event held Saturday on the same gorgeous lawn as the main Concours. Rather than a formal show this is a low-key gathering of 450 car guys and gals, with enthusiasts driving everything from Ferraris to hot rods, Mini Coopers and to Rolls Royce, Edsel station wagons to vintage race cars. It's a great time mixing with car lovers from every niche in the hobby. The show is free to spectators

My re-entry to the hobby would be as a participant in the Cars & Coffee event, my first go at what I considered to be a lofty gathering on the lawn of the Amelia Golf Club located in front of the Ritz Carlton. Should I leave the typical ball cap and T-shirt home? Do I need a tweed driving cap, maybe an ascot and blazer? At home, while detailing the W-motor in my '60 Corvette I wrestled with proper attire. In the end I blended in nicely a favorite ball cap and upscale automotive themed polo shirt.

The effects of Covid remained causing a bit less auction activity. The official auction of Amelia Island, RM-Sotheby was held in person, as was the Bonhams auction. This year the Thursday Gooding & Company auction was an online only affair, they plan to return to the big top in 2022. The good news for our hobby is sales were brisk with an over ninety percent sell-through at the onsite auctions.

ABOVE: Cars & Coffee at the Concours is held every year the day before the big concours event. Among this year's group was this very nice '34 Ford Woody.

BELOW: A fully restored '60 Corvette shares the C&C field with a nice hot rod '55 Chevy. While Chevrolet full size cars gave up the tooth grille in 1955, Corvettes showed their teeth until 1960.

OPPOSITE PAGE TOP: This 1932 Packard Convertible Victoria rides on a huge 147.5 inch wheelbase and under that long hood you will find a straight-eight displacing 385 cubic inches, good for 135 silky smooth horsepower. There was also a V-12 version of this car in '32. The Woodlite style headlights are occasionally seen on hot rods, but something we had never seen before is the matching parking lights atop the fenders.

OPPOSITE PAGE BOTTOM: This is one of 85 Cadillac Sport Phaetons built in 1930-31 on the V-16 chassis. The car was originally delivered to P.W. Harvey a multimillionaire industrial leader in Cleveland, Ohio. From the huge headlights to the split windshield and engine-turned dash this dual-cowl phaeton is filled with great hot rod ideas.

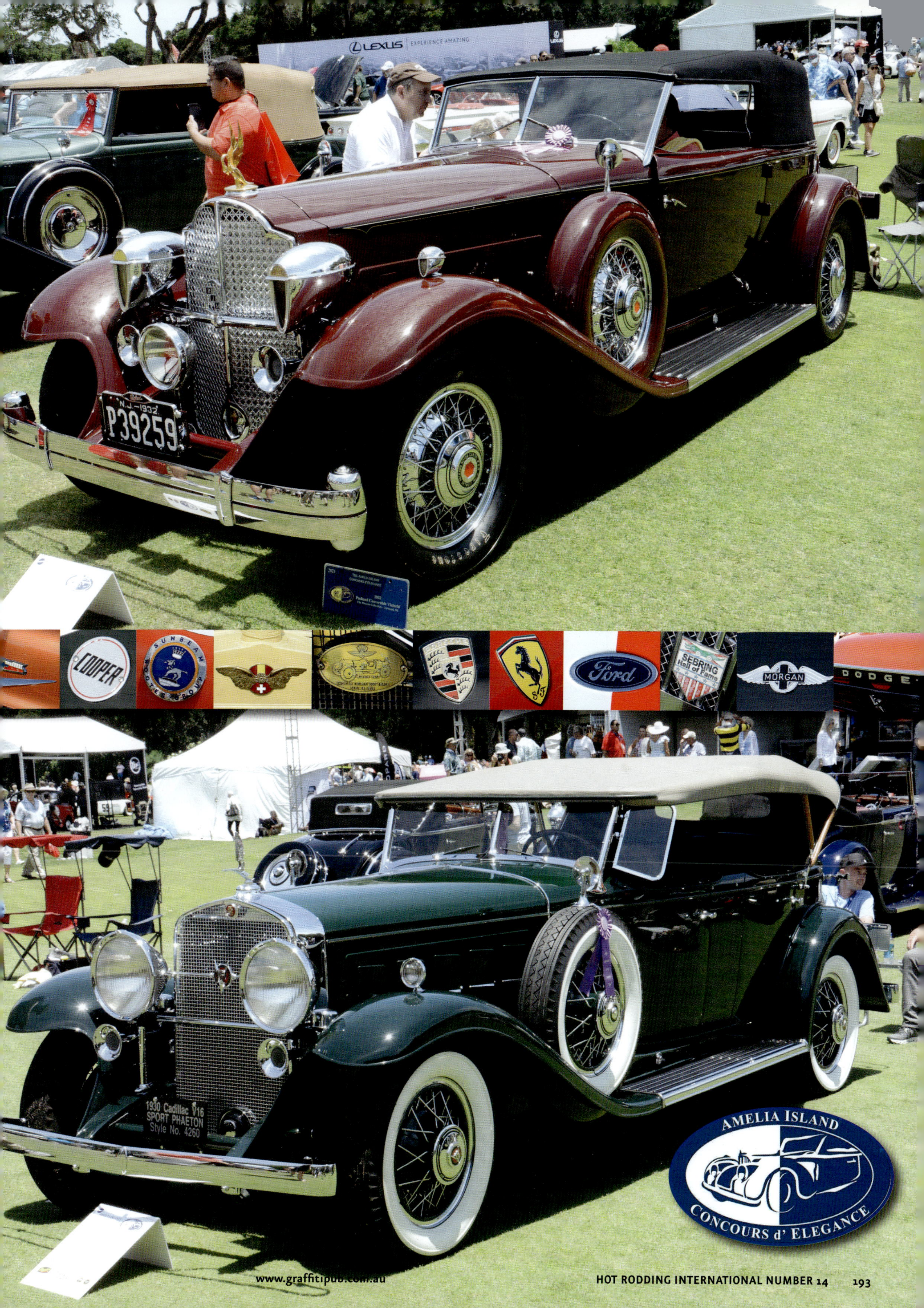

There were also seminars during the week with panels of automotive experts and luminaries. One such seminar was the Chevy Thunder Seminar with folks such as former director of Chevrolet Racing, Herb Fishel, Dale Earnhardt Jr., Ray Evernham among others on the panel.

Likewise, due to the COVID effect the Eight Flags Tour was smaller than usual, but no less diverse. Everything from supercars to a supercharged '57 Ford cruised the island before rolling into the scenic town of Fernandina Beach. The town closes the main street to provide parking for the great selection of vintage cars for the public to enjoy. This popular event will no doubt be back to full strength for 2022. While show fields are great, they pale in comparison to seeing and hearing a group of vintage cars motoring down a country road.

The Sunday Concours enjoyed perfect weather and the field was filled with amazing automobiles, but the best part is every car tells a story. It is these stories that provide the undercurrent of fun at the event. Selecting and soliciting a field of over three hundred cars this special is a tremendous amount of work for the organizers, with planning a year or more in advance.

Yes, from Hispano Suiza to Corvette race cars the field holds something for everyone and it is a great place to garner ideas for that project in your garage. Today's cellphone makes photographing ideas from classic cars and race cars simple. Need I remind you of things like the engine turned dashboard of the Auburn Speedster, or the beautifully scalloped paint on the fenders of a 1930 Ruxton? Did the classics influence the early hot rodders? Yes, beyond a doubt.

Reading the placards is both educational and entertaining. Speaking of education, you'll see and learn about cars you never knew existed. The show always contains special themes, this year they ranged from sections dedicated to everything from "Weird and Wonderful" to American Classics, Super Cars and European Exotics, Chevy Thunder to the Porsche 935. The 2021 show also traced the electric car, ranging from a 1912 Woods to a 2021 Cadillac Lyriq (and no, I don't know how to pronounce that name).

One of our favorite shows within the show is the fashion show. A small but entertaining group, it consists of models and owners dressed in period correct clothing as they ride/drive into the awards area. There was everything from a 1929 Mercedes Boat Tail roadster carrying a leather helmet, jacket and goggles clad lady to a 1970 Dodge Charger, resplendent in Panther Pink, with a lovely hippy-dippy-bell-bottomed-go-go-booted lady adding flair to an already outrageous muscle car. Yes, the fashion show is very cool and will continue to grow as it becomes a popular integral part of the show. All this contributes to the feeling that this is truly is a celebration and while the ribbons and awards are special the fun factor remains the best reward.

This year's Honoree was Lyn St. James, a racing lady who made her mark with class wins at the 24 Hours of Daytona, 12-Hours of Sebring and racing seven times in the Indy 500. A full display of the cars she raced was an impressive sight and a reminder that she was an incredibly versatile a driver. Today you can still find her behind the wheel at vintage race events.

Next year the 27th Amelia Island Concours d'Elegance will be held March 4-6. A special section celebrating ninety years of the 1932 Ford, including hot rods and rare originals is planned. While many believe Concours are for the elite, I think you will be pleasantly surprised to find a field filled with friendly people all sharing the common bond of loving the automobile. I heartily recommend you attend The Amelia… once done you may find yourself coming back for more. ■

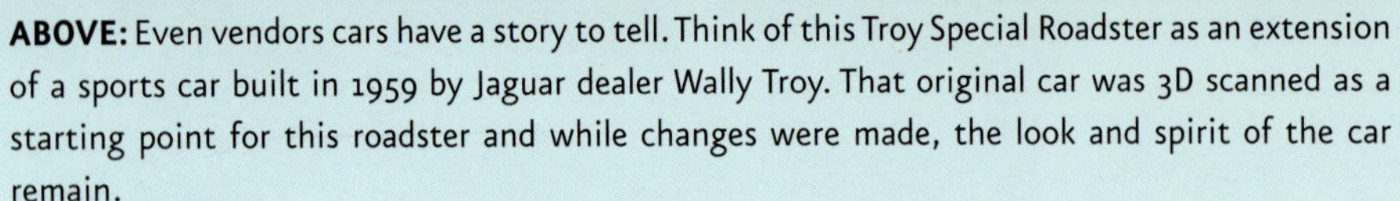

ABOVE: Even vendors cars have a story to tell. Think of this Troy Special Roadster as an extension of a sports car built in 1959 by Jaguar dealer Wally Troy. That original car was 3D scanned as a starting point for this roadster and while changes were made, the look and spirit of the car remain.

ABOVE RIGHT: Slide into the cockpit of the Troy Indy Special and you'll be sitting in drum-dyed European leather over custom formed aluminum bucket seats. A wood grained Nardi wheel is period perfect and the Wings Series Stewart-Warner gauges fill the aluminum dash. Custom seat sliders provide leg room to fit people over six feet tall. The car Wally Troy built had a tubular frame and aluminum body powered by a dual-quad 283 Chevy motor. The new Troy Indy Special from 7fifteen Motors also has a tube frame, beautifully formed aluminum body and a potent 495-HP, LS3 engine. With a curb weight of 2200 pounds this should be an exhilarating roadster. Only 33 Troy Indy Specials will be built.

ABOVE: Cars and Coffee has something for everybody, you could say it takes a village or in this case an Edsel Villager station wagon towing a period correct camper both looking good in red and white. It was a real crowd pleaser.

RIGHT: One of our favorites of the show was this 1929 Mercedes-Benz S Barker Tourer. The name is almost as long as the car. Those torpedoes under the doors are compartments for tools and spares and flow perfectly with the boattail design. Polished aluminum panels combine with the 1929 rich blue paint inspired by the color of peacock feathers on an 1850 dress. Matching contoured luggage and a young lady dressed in period attire complete the image.

ABOVE: This gorgeous 1939 Ford Woodie rolled into the C&C event and was parked next to a modern version, the Jeep Wagoneer. While we are not sure what is under the hood, externally the '39 Woodie remains stock.

RIGHT: This British Racing Green Morgan was a standout in a full row of Morgans. This is a modern Morgan as the company still produces approximately 800 handcrafted cars per year in Malvern, UK.

BELOW: Making it's Concours debut was this, one of seven, 1953 Maverick Sportsters. Designed by Sterling "Smoke" Gladwin Jr., the fiberglass bodied boulevard sports car is recognized as America's last production boattail speedster. This was Gladwin's personal car, built on a '40 LaSalle chassis. The later six production cars were built on a postwar Cadillac chassis with Caddy 331 V-8 power.

 So you want to go vintage racing? Well jump in a set of coveralls, strap on a leather helmet with goggles and lean down behind the circular windshield. Rock hard narrow tires connect you to the pavement. It took a real man to hang on to these early racers. Judging by the modern header wrap this car still sees some driving.

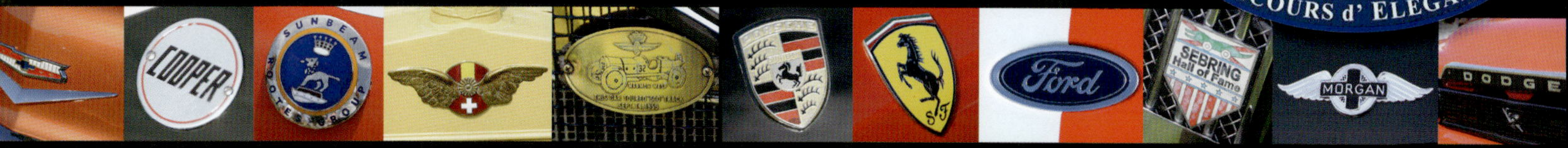

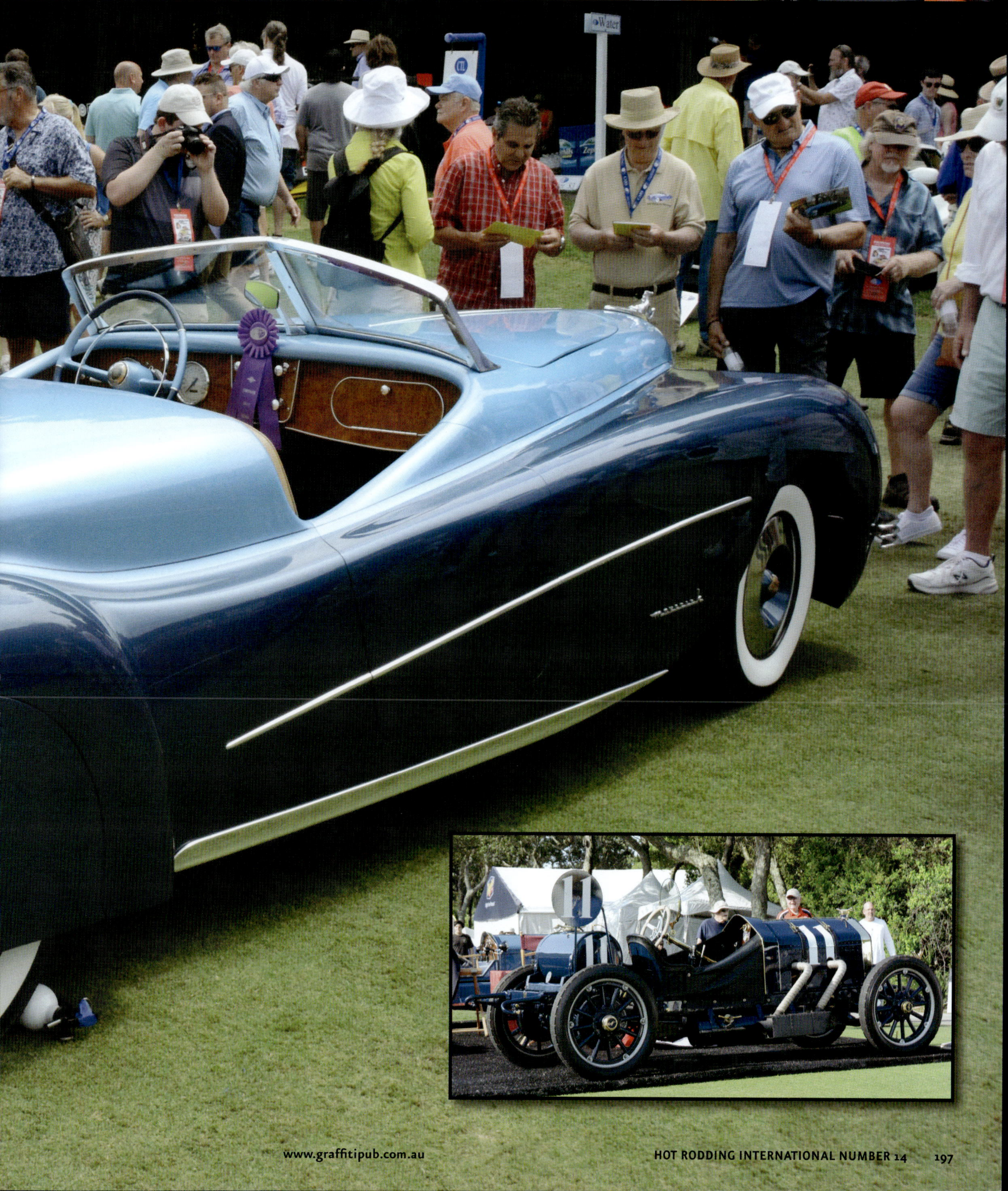

LEFT: This '57 Ford Custom Tudor was found in a shed in Tennessee in 1965 by then 13-year-old Richard Stuck. He purchased the car for $150.00 and brought it home to New Jersey. The car was purported to have run some "shine" in the fifties. Richard had the car running in time for high school but later realized the "F" in the VIN signified this was one of just 250 F-code, factory supercharged, full-size Fords produced in 1957.

BELOW: While restoration began in 2011, it took seven years to find all the proper pieces with restoration of the '57 Custom completed in 2018. The meticulous engine bay includes all proper factory stampings and finishes. Note the dual V-belts on the blower, just finding those proper pulleys is a feat itself. The car was originally prepared by Ford to compete at Bonneville Land Speed Trials but it never raced due to the AMA ban on racing. Period correct decals add to the charm of this flawless Ford and yes, Richard Stuck still owns the car. He did a good job picking his first car.

LEFT & BELOW: BNC (Bollack-Netteret Cie) only manufactured cars from 1923-31. This 1930 Roadster has history back to 1943 when George Caswell purchased the car. It was SCCA raced extensively with the historic podium finish at the 1948 Watkins Glen Junior Gran Prix. The car went through a series of owners before being parked in 1970. It sat covered in various garages until 2008 when Peter McLaughlin purchased and restored it.

ABOVE: For the uninitiated the Auburn dash is not some reproduction piece designed for hot rods. Here we find the famed Auburn dash in its natural habitat… inside an actual Auburn Boattail Speedster. The elegant simplicity of classic car dashboards works well in hot rods.

RIGHT: You just can't gather a great group of gearheads without a healthy group of Porsches. From the 911 to the 914 and Boxster they were all on hand for Cars & Coffee. This Aubergine Cabriolet is a fine example in one of our favorite colors.

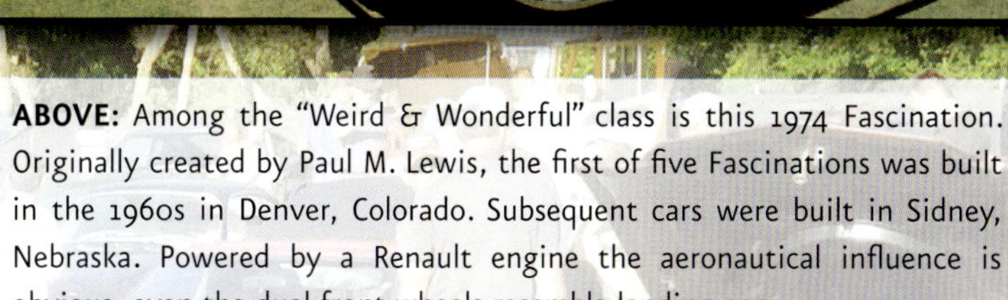

ABOVE: Rambler and Lincoln were the only two American auto manufacturers to undergo complete restyling in 1956. The public loved it and Lincoln sales doubled. The Premier was the top-of-the-line Lincoln based on the Futura show car (later to become the Batmobile). In '56 Lincoln called the Premier "the longest, lowest, most powerful, most wanted Lincoln of all time."

ABOVE: Among the "Weird & Wonderful" class is this 1974 Fascination. Originally created by Paul M. Lewis, the first of five Fascinations was built in the 1960s in Denver, Colorado. Subsequent cars were built in Sidney, Nebraska. Powered by a Renault engine the aeronautical influence is obvious, even the dual front wheels resemble landing gear.

ABOVE: The author's '60 Corvette arrived early for the Cars & Coffee. Under the hood a 348 cubic inch "W-motor" is fed by twin FAST injectors, begging the question, what if Chevrolet had built a big block Corvette in 1960? Once a drag car, the Corvette is the result of a three-year homebuilt effort.

ABOVE: Don't be too quick to judge the Judge. This is one of just 325 Ram Air IV, four speed examples of the 1970 GTO Judge. The Orbit Orange paint is pure '70s. The original motor is still under the hood with 400 cubic inches good for 370 HP and mid-13s in the quarter mile. Pontiac advertisements had catch lines like "The Judge can be bought."

BELOW & BELOW RIGHT: The 1939 Alfa Romeo 8C 2900B coupe evokes the image of speed and style. The car had plenty of both with the race version winning the Mille Miglia. As hot rodders, we can see plenty of great ideas here, from the driving lights to the curvaceous bumpers and laid back grille. Less than forty of these cars were built. From the rear the graceful lines of the '39 Alfa combine aerodynamics with powerful style. Wrap around bumpers lead to ventilated skirts on huge teardrop rear fenders. The basic shape of the roof and rear window resemble the '63 split window Corvette.

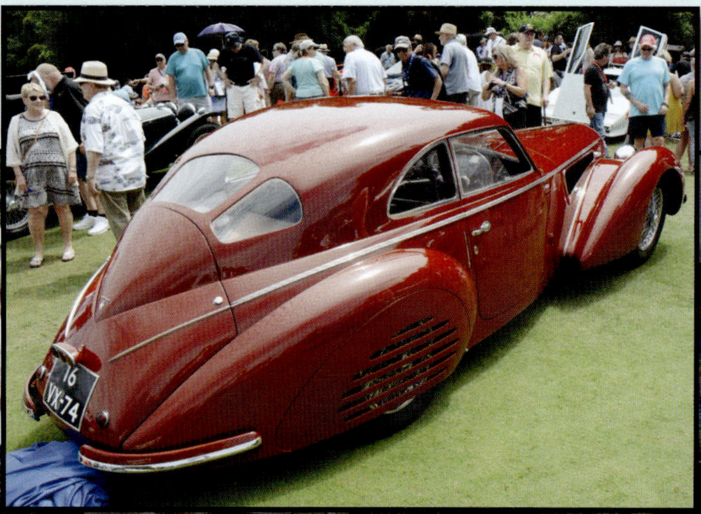

ABOVE LEFT: This '56 Chevrolet 210 was right at home on the lawn. Clean and simple always works on a Tri-five Chevy. We were taken by the diversity in cars and people. The common thread was simply the love of all things automotive.

LEFT: This 1960 Ewing Indianapolis Roadster is the work of Wayne "Fat Boy" Ewing, one of the more colorful characters of the '60s Indy roadster era. The Joe Hunt Magneto Special raced at Indy in 1960. At some point the car was converted to a super modified before being rescued and returned to Indy car specs by Roger Beck. The original graphics on the car were designed by Joe Hunt's fourteen year old son.

RIGHT: Just over 100 Harrington Alpines were produced in 1961. Thomas Harrington Ltd was a coach builder of bus bodies. The Harrington coupe fastback was designed by bus designer Ron Humphries. This car competed in the 1961 24 Hours of Le Mans and the 1962 12 Hours of Sebring. A year later, after a change of livery and a new owner, the car finished fourth in class at Sebring.

RIGHT: This 1956 Cooper T39 MKII Bobtail racer is one of 13 known survivors out of the 39 cars built. An instant success on the track, drivers like Michael MacDowell, Sir Stirling Moss and Sir Jack Brabham all drove Cooper Bobtails. This little race car changed the face of motor racing by moving the engine to the rear, and like so many '50s racers, it was done with a sense of style.

ABOVE: Among the cars rolling onto the lawn for the "fashion show" was this 1948 Tasco Prototype. The aircraft influence after WWII was everywhere and from the fully skirted wheels to the cockpit-style plexiglass canopy that influence shows. This car is credited with being the first T-top car and the first car to use magnesium wheels. Gordon Buehrig designed the car, it was never raced and never saw production.

RIGHT: From the front the Tasco appears ready to take flight. Large vertical grille and monstrous air intakes that house the headlights dominate the front end. The fenders are fiberglass, a totally new material in 1948.

GASSERS 7

August 28, 2021 10am-4pm

Words: Larry O'Toole
Photos: Paul Northey

Automobile Driving Museum
EL SEGUNDO, CALIFORNIA, USA

ABOVE: Willys pickups were popular as Gassers and no wonder when they look this good. Perched in the engine bay of this blue example is a supercharged big block Ford engine and a set of polished Halibrand style wheels add a touch of class.

LEFT: Also popular were the tiny English Popular or Anglia two door sedans. This one has a blown big block Chevy on board so the "Panic Attack" name seems quite appropriate. Cragar SS wheels are right in keeping for the era, along with extensive pinstriping and typical nose-up attitude. The tilt front gives easy engine access and it sports a cool set of fenderwell headers. Can you hear it?

The Automobile Driving Museum in El Segundo holds regular car shows out the front of its building that usually have an underlying theme. The Gassers 7 Rev Fest at the ADM was held on Auguat 28, 2021 with exhibitors' cars rolling in from 8:00am to take advantage of the first-come, first-serve parking. Gassers 7 was open to all drag car clubs and solo riders of the era; all coming together to celebrate Vintage Speed and Style!

A raffle, food trucks, vendors and awards were also part of the one day show with emcee "Hot Rod" Bob Beck introducing a host of guest speakers including Ed "Isky Iskenderian, Robert "Bones" Balogh, Jerry Mallicoat, Bob Muravez, Steve Gibbs and "Fast Jack" Beckman.

TOP RIGHT: Nagel Racing's "Crimson Ghost"'56 Chevy 210 sedan displays a high quality finish, a set of Doug's headers dumping from the fenderwell and it has been relieved of the front bumper to save weight.

ABOVE: No, this one isn't a Model A Ford, maybe a Chrysler product that demonstrates a superb standard of finish, is powered by a monstrous blown Hemi engine with wild zoomie headers and runs highly polished 12 spoke front wheels.

RIGHT: There were even some neat street rods that came along for a look at the Gassers, including this nicely finished '47 Ford woody wagon.

GASSERS 7

ABOVE: Who would have thought a four door Model A sedan could be a Gasser? The Sevillano Bros and Padilla Model A that is now owned by Dennis Jones was raced at Southern California dragstrips from 1966-'69. Blown small block Chevy engine, Cragar SS wheels and straight axle front end are all straight from that period. Note the small black and white photos of the car in action back then leaning against the front wheels.

LEFT: "High and Mighty" is an unusual '50 Plymouth three window Business Coupe with all the typical gasser tricks – tinted orange perspex in the door windows, jacked up front end, Moon tank out front and fenderwell headers dumping from a big block Chevy engine. The magazine on the windshield indicates it was a Hot Rod cover car back in its racing days. Cragar SS wheels would have been the latest thing when it was built for the track.

ABOVE: Looks like there's a 390 big block under the hood of "Demented", an uncommon '54 Ford two door Ranch Wagon decorated with panel painting and pinstripes. Leaving the front bumper off for racing was a popular measure to save pounds and increase weight transfer to the rear wheels.

LEFT: Tommy Ivo was around the drag racing scene right from the early days in California when slingshot dragsters all looked like this one. Hoop roll bars, full body and long zoomie headers were all typical, but Ivo was a little different to most in using Buick Nailhead engines in his drag cars, this one with fuel injection before it became common. Who could have imagined slingshot dragsters like this one would evolve into the beasts we see at the drag strips today?

ABOVE: Another set of those popular Cragar SS wheels on this '37 Chevy coupe gasser that's motivated by a small block V8.

ABOVE: The blown Hemi engine would certainly wake up this aged Model A Tudor from Nachos Upholstery.

ABOVE: Powder blue Thunderbird is a desirable collector car turned gasser with 289 Ford engine and five spoke mag wheels. The "Surfin Bird" has twin four barrel carbies on the engine and a Moon tank out front.

LEFT: Kaiser built Henry Js were popular as gassers thanks to their smaller size and light weight. Leaving the front bumper off made them lighter again and a jacked up front end gave them good weight transfer for better traction off the line.

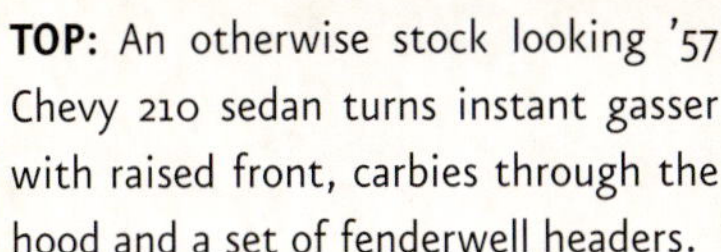

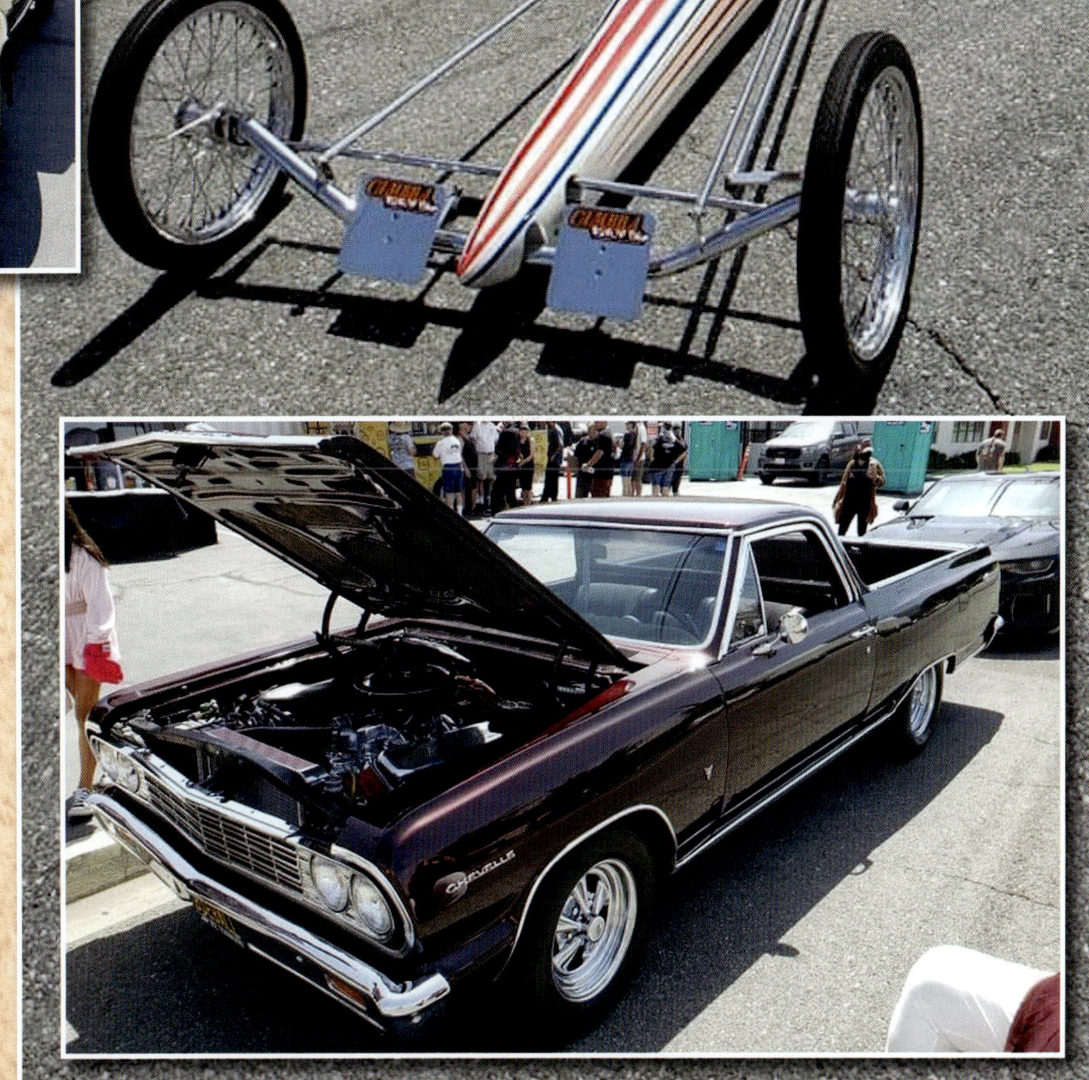

TOP: An otherwise stock looking '57 Chevy 210 sedan turns instant gasser with raised front, carbies through the hood and a set of fenderwell headers.

ABOVE RIGHT: Beautiful Top Fuel slingshot dragster from Dean Engineering is a study in symmetry and design that makes you want to go back to the late sixties. The blown Hemi only adds to the mystique.

ABOVE: They weren't very big so Ford Populars were often turned int gassers too. Their short wheelbase often made handling precarious and this one sports an injected Hemi engine, so it would have been a real handful.

RIGHT: Another visiting spectator vehicle, this time a really nice Chevy El Camino in pearl purple with another set of those popular Cragar SS wheels.

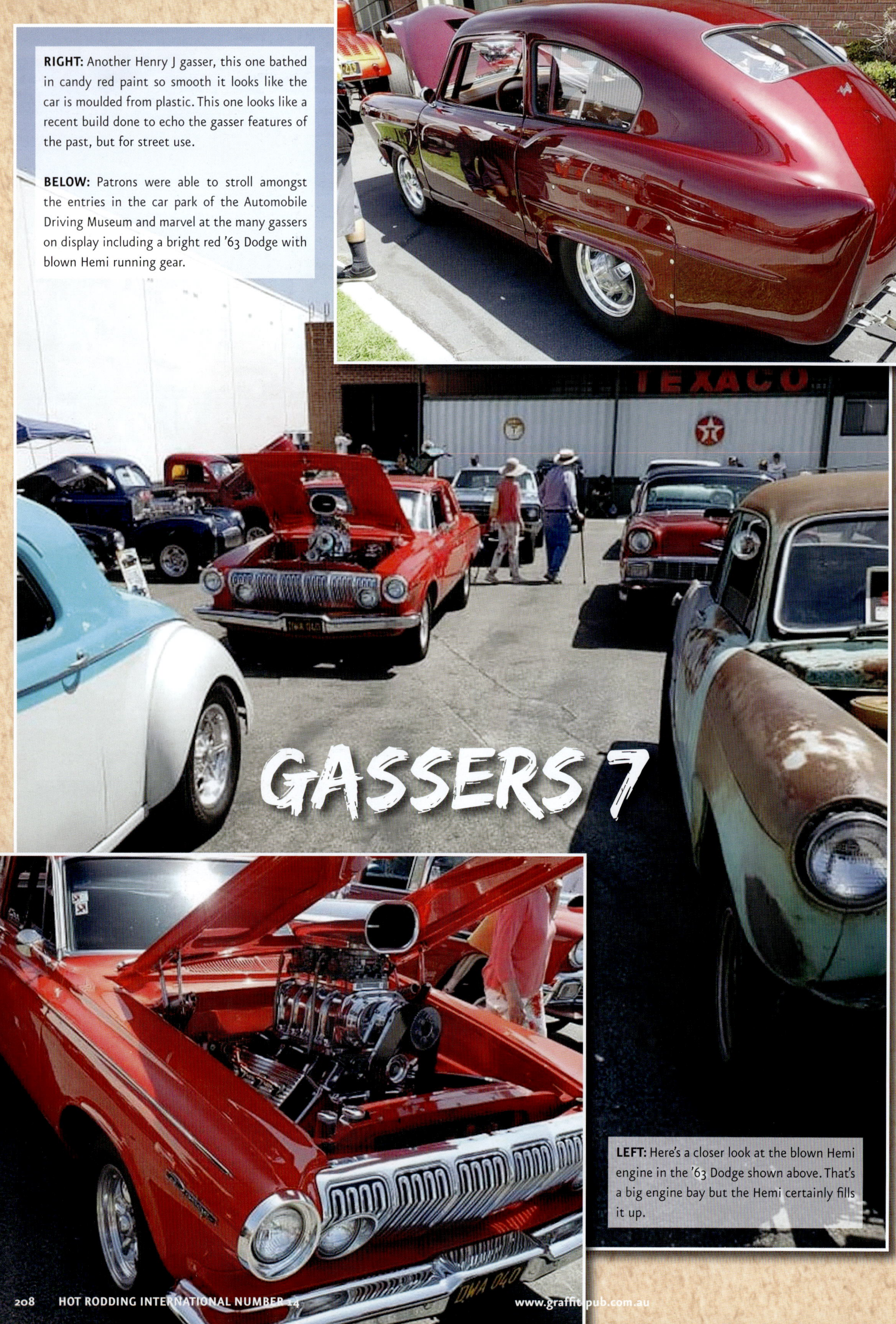

RIGHT: Another Henry J gasser, this one bathed in candy red paint so smooth it looks like the car is moulded from plastic. This one looks like a recent build done to echo the gasser features of the past, but for street use.

BELOW: Patrons were able to stroll amongst the entries in the car park of the Automobile Driving Museum and marvel at the many gassers on display including a bright red '63 Dodge with blown Hemi running gear.

GASSERS 7

LEFT: Here's a closer look at the blown Hemi engine in the '63 Dodge shown above. That's a big engine bay but the Hemi certainly fills it up.